all about
himalayan cats

joan mcdonald brearley

Cover:
Ch. Tailspin Jupiter of Harobed, owned by Rose Levy of Plainview, New York. Photo by Miceli Studios, Ltd.

Frontispiece:
Copplestone Betianne, bred and owned by Mrs. I. Bentinck, Copplestone Cattery, Berkshire, England.

ISBN 0-87666-850-3

© Copyright 1976 by T.F.H. Publications, Inc. Ltd.

Distributed in the U.S.A. by T.F.H. Publications, Inc., 211 West Sylvania Avenue, P.O. Box 27, Neptune City, N.J. 07753; in England by T.F.H. (Gt. Britain) Ltd., 13 Nutley Lane, Reigate, Surrey; in Canada to the book store and library trade by Clarke, Irwin & Company, Clarwin House, 791 St. Clair Avenue West, Toronto 10, Ontario; in Canada to the pet trade by Rolf C. Hagen Ltd., 3225 Sartelon Street, Montreal 382, Quebec; in Southeast Asia by Y.W. Ong, 9 Lorong 36 Geylang, Singapore 14; in Australia and the South Pacific by Pet Imports Pty. Ltd., P.O. Box 149, Brookvale 2100, N.S.W., Australia. Published by T.F.H. Publications, Inc., Ltd., The British Crown Colony of Hong Kong.

TABLE OF CONTENTS

4

Acknowledgements

The author acknowledges with thanks the co-operation of all the Himalayan owners who so willingly submitted photographs of their beautiful cats for presentation in this book . . . to Richard Gebhardt for his strong encouragement and valued friendship over the years . . . to Mrs. S. M. Harding, England, for selling me my treasured Himalayans . . . to Robert R. Shomer, DVM, for expert counsel . . . and to Jane Levy for showing us how to bathe Himalayans.

Very special thanks are due to Rose Levy, whose friendship I value highly, and whose enthusiasm and unselfish advice introduced me to the breed which has given me so much enjoyment for so many years.

Dedication

In loving memory of Mingchiu Manderin of Sahadi, champion in England, Scotland, Wales, and the United States, and Mingchiu Nita, Mandella and Giselle, all of which shared my life and my love for all too short a time . . . but helped endear this marvelous breed to me forever!

*"Those who'll play with cats
must expect to be scratched."*

from *Don Quixote*

ABOUT THE AUTHOR

JOAN MCDONALD BREARLEY

Joan Brearley has loved animals ever since she was old enough to know what they were. Over the years there has been a constant succession of dogs, cats, birds, fish, rabbits, snakes, turtles, alligators, squirrels, lizards, etc., for her own personal menagerie. Through these same years she has owned over thirty different breeds of pure-bred dogs, as well as countless mixtures, since the door was never closed to a needy or homeless animal.

A graduate of the American Academy of Dramatic Arts, Joan started her career as a writer for movie magazines and as an actress and dancer. She also studied journalism at Columbia University and has been a radio, TV and magazine writer, writing for some of the major New York agencies. She also has been producer-director for a major network.

Through the years she has owned and/or bred Himalayans, Siamese, Rex, Abyssinians, Egyptians, Persians, Burmese, and Domestic Shorthairs, as well as over thirty different breeds of purebred dogs. Since 1973 she has been Editor of the *Cat Fanciers Association Yearbook* and has written articles on cats for various magazines. She is very interested in animal legislation and speaks at kennel and cat clubs and humane organizations on the subject. She has received many awards and citations for her work in this field.

Her accomplishments in the dog fancy include becoming an American Kennel Club judge and a breeder-exhibitor of top show dogs, and she is the author of more than a dozen dog breed books. Joan bred a Westminster Kennel Club Group winner in her first litter of Afghan Hounds, Champion Sahadi (her kennel and cattery prefix) Shikari, for many years the top-winning Afghan Hound in the history of the breed. For five years she was Executive Vice President of the Popular Dogs Publishing Company and editor of *Popular Dogs* magazine, the national prestige publication for the dog fancy at that time.

At present Joan lives in a penthouse apartment overlooking Manhattan with a dozen or more cats, a Shih Tzu, Cavalier King Charles Spaniel and a Pug, many of which are Best in Show winners and have been professional models for television and magazines. In addition to her activities in the world of animals Joan Brearley is a movie buff and spends time at the art and auction galleries, the theatre, creating needlepoint (for which she has also won awards,) dancing, the typewriter — and the zoo!

Chapter 1

THE BEAUTIFUL HIMALAYANS

No other cat in the history of the cat fancy has so captured the admiration of cat lovers the way the Himalayan has! Siamese in color, Persian in type and combining the best qualities of both breeds in one magnificent creature, the "rare new breed" has endeared itself to all people who profess to love cats . . . .

A CASE OF MISTAKEN IDENTITY

Since the 1950's, when the Himalayan cat began to come more and more into the public eye, more and more of an educational program has had to be conducted in order to educate the public as to just what a Himalayan cat is. In the beginning, they were thought to be longhair Siamese. Nothing — but *nothing* — infuriates the Himalayan fanciers more than that misnomer!

The Himalayan is NOT a longhair Siamese. In fact, a longhair Siamese is a Balinese, another breed entirely. A Himalayan cat is a Persian cat with the color pattern of the Siamese cat.

True, in the beginning the breed was created by breeding a Persian to a Siamese, but only to pick up the Himalayan (or Siamese) coat color pattern, nothing more. The only thing "Siamese" about the Himalayan is the color pattern, and once that was established there has been no further need to go back to the Siamese breed for any reason whatsoever.

Opposite:
Triple Champion Mingchiu Nita of Sahadi, English import Blue Point Himalayan which won the 1965 *Cats Magazine* Award as Eastern Honorable Mention Blue Point Himalayan Female. Owned by Joan Brearley, Sahadi Cattery, New York City. Born August, 1963; the sire was Briarry Valparago *ex* Briarry Suzannah.

WHAT IS A HIMALAYAN?

The Himalayan is expected to resemble, in every way, a Persian cat. It must have a cobby body, short, strong legs, short tail, flat face, massive head, large round eyes, small widespread ears and long, luxurient coat. In addition to the outward appearances, the disposition and temperament of the Himalayan is expected to be as completely Persian as possible: voice, placid behavior, and complete companionability.

WHAT IS THE HIMALAYAN COLOR PATTERN?

The Siamese cat is known for its light body color with dark points, points being dark coloration on face, ears, tail, feet and legs. It is this color pattern that is known as the Himalayan color pattern because it is found on rabbits, goats, etc., originally found in the area around the Himalayan Mountains in Asia. Therefore, it is a Himalayan, not Siamese, color pattern.

HOW A HIMALAYAN CAT IS PRODUCED

The Himalayan cat is one of the comparatively few breeds of domesticated animals for which a complete and verifiable history of origin is known. A cat with long hair and bearing the Himalayan color pattern can be produced within a few generations of breeding, as is shown in a later section.

Since self-color is dominant to the Siamese color pattern and short hair is dominant to long hair, the hybrid result between a Siamese and Persian will be shorthaired self-colored kittens. The mating of two such black or blue hybrids will produce some kittens with both long hair and Siamese coloring. Since these two characteristics are genetically recessive, cats showing them will breed true when bred to other cats showing the same characteristics. But in the beginning improvement in type was achieved by a considerable amount of outcrossing to solid-color longhaired black and blue Persians. Some of the best breeding developed from mating unrelated Himalayans to the self-colored cats carrying colorpoint genes ᴎo insure the Persian body-type.

Today there is such good breeding stock available through established lines that it is no longer necessary to go back to Persian or Siamese breeding stock. Our Himalayan cats today continue to improve on all points, and some truly magnificent specimens are being seen and are winning top honors at the cat show.

Champion Cat Lore Cupid, Blue Point male photographed at a show at 18 months of age. Bred and owned by Laurie Stevens Cat Lore Cattery, Chicago, Illinois.

Chapter 2

THE CREATION
OF THE HIMALAYAN
IN AMERICA

Miss Virginia Cobb and Dr. Clyde Keeler were among the very first to create what is now known as the Himalayan cat in the United States. Breedings of the Siamese/Persian cross had undoubtedly been tried; among those making the attempt was Mrs. Flossielu Beer in Colorado, but it was Virginia Cobb who actually possessed the foresight to see the potential in the magnificent blending of the two most popular breeds.

Miss Cobb, who was associated with the Howe Laboratory at Harvard Medical School and active in the Siamese Cat Society of America, wrote an article for the September, 1936 issue of *The Journal of Heredity* describing the ultimate creation of the Himalayan cat. In 1930, Dr. Clyde Keeler, an instructor at the Harvard Medical School and Fellow of the Bussey Institution of Harvard, approached Miss Cobb at a Boston cat show. He asked her if she would be interested in conducting some experimental cross-breeding between Siamese and Persian cats with the idea of developing a new breed.

Virginia Cobb told him she would be *very* interested. At this initial meeting they discussed the fact that it would involve many years of time and many breedings and that they must determine whether the Siamese pattern was recessive and whether the long hair on the Persian was recessive also. As early as 1927 doubts had been expressed about the inheritance factors in the Siamese coat-color, even after additional work had been done after Dr. T. Tjebbes' 1924 report in Sweden stating that it

Copplestone Besta, photographed as a kitten at the cattery of her breeder, Mrs. I. Bentinck, Berkshire, England. Besta now lives with her new owner in Sweden.

Mingchiu Souk photographed at 8 months of age with the ribbons of just one show! Bred and owned by Mrs. S. M. Harding of England.

was not at all understood, and that "it must be confessed that the evidence is not very full" regarding long hair as being a recessive. No mention of any longhaired Siamese recombinations had been made, but blacks, whites and tabby Siamese had resulted from the cross of White Persian to Siamese made by Tjebbes. Cobb and Keeler also realized that all the cats they used must be of pedigreed stock if the new breed was ever to take hold in the fancy.

So their experiments began. They first crossed a Siamese female with a Silver Persian male. Three shorthaired Silver Tabby kittens resulted. Then a Siamese female was mated with a Smoke Persian male. Seven shorthaired Smoke kittens were produced. In 1931 a Siamese female was mated to a Black Persian male. As a result of this mating, three shorthaired Black kittens were born. These crosses, all of which are recorded with illustrations and photographs, were published in the May, 1933 issue of *The Journal of Heredity*.

From the last mating, Siamese to Black Persian, a male was

Peek-a-boo! Two of Mrs. S. M. Harding's kittens peek over the edge of their bed. Mrs. Harding's Mingchiu Cattery is in England.

selected. They chose the one with the most wave in the coat to be used for future breedings. He was named Newton's Bozo. In 1932 a Black Persian female, Ch. Newton's Susannah, was bred to a Siamese male named Ch. Newton's Sy Mingo. The result was a litter of two shorthaired kittens, both black, one male and one female. The female was kept for breeding and named Newton's Bitzie.

In 1933 the shorthaired hybrid, Bitzie, was mated to Bozo. The litter contained a longhaired black female named Newton's Babbit. This cat, mated back to her sire, Bozo, produced five kittens: two standard pattern Siamese, two black longhairs and one of Siamese pattern whose coat looked a bit different from those of her two Siamese sisters. At ten days of age, this kitten indicated that she would be a kitten with long hair! It was a very exciting day for Virginia Cobb and Dr. Keeler. Their six years of work had ended successfully! The first Himalayan kitten was named Debutante.

Virginia Cobb stated: "Entirely aside from any credit due for my years of hard work, the most *credit* should go to Dr. Keeler for his vision in 1930 and his scientific knowledge that made all of his predictions 100% accurate." Present day Himalayan breeders still have a great respect for Dr. Keeler's work and advice.

Miss Cobb had no intention of continuing the breeding of the Himalayan cats; she had just wanted the thrill of actually producing one, for actually she was a dedicated Siamese breeder. All of the Keeler/Cobb progress was published regarding the new breed, since never at any time had there been any secret about what they were trying to accomplish. They had been in correspondence with Richard Hayden Hood, who had been mentioned as an early breeder of Himalayans. He did have Siamese cats with long hair, but he did not know how they were produced, nor were his of pedigreed stock. Mr. Hood had Silver Persians and Siamese cats cohabiting, and this "new breed" was a natural result. In photographs sent to Miss Cobb by Mr. Hood it was evident that some of the kittens had white toes, and an article about Mr. Hood's cats in *Cats Magazine* further stated that they had webbed front feet. Silver carries both black and white color, so white could understandably have appeared on these Siamese.

Other friends of Virginia Cobb and Dr. Keeler who allowed them to use their studs as outcrosses were Mrs. Emma Raymond, whose Ch. Sambo was used, and Mrs. Mabel La Fayette, who donated the use of her Ch. Tamson. All the other studs were from Virginia Cobb's Newton Cattery. But they were also grateful to their many friends who gave homes to the many kittens resulting from their research project.

Grand Champion Nevah-Tep's Vogue, Seal Point female bred and owned by Larry Keely and Boris Teron of Chicago, Illinois.

Following a short and tragic illness, Virginia Cobb died on November 20, 1969. Highly esteemed in the world of cats not only for her tireless and productive research but also for her genuine love of the individual cats, she made a very prophetic statement that still holds true today. In a "Message from the President" column in the *Siamese Cat Society of America* publication, she stated in her closing remarks (after finishing her third term as its highest officer): "In closing I want to add a personal wish for the Seal Point Siamese cat of the future; that is, that these cats return to the light fawn body which they *used*

17

to have. Even with perfect type it is *color* which makes the Siamese cat." The author agrees that it is the Himalayan color pattern that makes the Himalayan cat what it is, and we can now be grateful that we can have our beautiful contrasting colors as well as body type and conformation in our Himalayans less than half a century after Virginia Cobb and Clyde Keeler pioneered in the breed.

There is no denying the Himalayan cat started with Virginia Cobb, and the *American Journal of Heredity* credits her for this achievement. Her "Newton" Siamese cattery name was known throughout the world, and she was selling quality kittens until very shortly before her death. Countless memorial trophies and cat shows were dedicated to her memory after her death, and proceeds from the establishment of the Virginia R. Cobb Memorial Fund were forwarded to the Morris Animal Foundation for research into the diseases of cats.

OTHER EARLY BREEDERS

After World War II the Himalayan started to come into its own, when Marguerita Goforth in the U.S.A. and Mr. Brian Stirling-Webb in England took the breed beyond the self-color stage and presented an eager public with the Himalayan cat with its transmissible characteristics which set it apart as a "new breed."

One of the first and one of the most influential proponents of the Himalayan cat was Marguerita Goforth of San Diego, California. Beginning in 1950 she spared neither time nor expense to get the breed started and established in the fancy. It took her over 10 years of slow development to bring the breed up to the quality and beauty necessary to capture the interest of the public.

When asked what was involved in originating her new breed, Mrs. Goforth said, "The answer is many years of selective line breeding, many cages, many cats, moments of discouragement and times when the breeder wonders if it is worth the tremendous amount of work, expense and worry. There are many discards, poor type, wrong color, etc. for several generations. And homes for these must be found where they will not be used for breeding purposes. Then comes the final step and proof that you have actually originated a new breed. This is when official recognition by the cat association is achieved. Until one receives this official recognition he has not developed a breed. Simple crosses do not make a breed. One thing, and one thing only — official recognition by the associations — makes a new breed a reality. This can only be accomplished when the cats conform to a type and breed true, and this takes years of breeding with a plan, "a blue print" of what the ideal cat should be."

Marguerita Goforth used White, Blue and Black in her original breeding program for the Himalayans. Most prominent as a stud force was her Blue Persian Delphi Blue Splendor of Goforth, bred by Mrs. Fannie Mood. Splendor was

Seal Point Himalayan Copplestone Justin and a friend. Photographed by Thomas Fall for owner Mrs. I. Bentinck, Berkshire, England.

a son of Lavender Mischiefmaker and sired many outstanding show cats in his day.

As a child, Mrs. Goforth had had Blue-eyed Whites (called Angoras then) and over the years added all colors of Siamese, Persians, Manx and eventually the Himalayan to her cattery. She is also a judge of cats and has officiated all over the U.S.A. including Hawaii, and she was on the panel of the 50th Anniversary show of the Boston Cat Club. In private life she was an artist and sculptress specializing in animals; she designed various cats for the Dodge Trophy Company which still adorn many of the trophies given as prizes at the shows.

Mrs. Goforth became very active in the International Himalayan Society when it was one of the first clubs created for owners of Himalayans and dedicated to the education of the public on the advantages of the breed as well as a dedication to breeding the cat true to the Standard.

Since the popularity of the Himalayan has grown to such major proportions there has been a great deal of controversy as to whether the cat is a Persian in the true sense of the word. Mrs. Goforth believed that it was *not* a Persian, just a cat of Persian *type*, and was a breed unto itself. A longhair. In 1959 she wrote:

"One article I recently read states that the Himalayan is not a longhaired Siamese but is a Persian. The first statement is quite correct, since we are breeding for a cobby Persian type with Siamese coloring *only*. The second statement is in error, for neither is the Himalayan a Persian. If it were, there could be no Siamese blood in it, and thus no Siamese color. No, the Himalayan is neither Siamese nor Persian but is an entirely new breed of Longhair. In other words, we now have two breeds of Longhairs — Persians and Himalayans, just as we have several breeds of Shorthairs, none of which are divisions of other breeds but distinct breeds in themselves."

On the other hand, Virginia Cobb wrote in October, 1965: "I have felt for many years that the Himalayan cat should be recognized as a color of Longhair. All breeders of Himalayans recognize that in order to keep the wanted type, a Persian must be introduced. One must sacrifice color for type, else in a short time the Himalayan will have the long nose, slanted eyes, etc., of the Siamese."

And so the controversy raged. However, once the Himalayan was recognized by all of the cat associations for exhibiting in the championship classes, the breed was listed as a breed of Longhair with no tolerance of breeding back to the Persians or the Siamese. It is now the opinion of virtually everyone that the breed is established and the need for further outcrosses is unnecessary and unacceptable to the governing bodies of the cat fancy in this country.

Ch. X.O.X. Betula and her daughter Copplestone Maria. Maria has two C.C.'s. This photograph is one which appeared in the book *Champion Cats of the World.* Owned by Mrs. I. Bentinck, Copplestone Cattery, Berkshire, England.

THE FIRST HIMALAYAN TO BE EXHIBITED

In November, 1957 Marguerita Goforth exhibited her Goforth's Winsome Lass and Goforth's Prince Hopeful at the Silvergate Cat Club show in San Diego. Mrs. Goforth's friend, Mr. Price Cross, President of the newly formed American Cat Fanciers Association, raved over the breed and did not hesitite when Mrs. Goforth asked him if he could get Himalayans recognized by the ACFA. He felt that he could, and Mrs. Goforth presented him with a pair of kittens so that he could show them to the ACFA Executive Council meeting that December. These kittens were Goforth's Don Diego and Goforth's La Chiquita. La Chiquita became the first Himalayan champion in the United States.

Triple Champion Mingchiu Nita of Sahadi and her sister Mingchiu Rissa photographed in England in November of 1963 at three and one-half months of age. Nita, imported by Joan Brearley, was a Blue Point; Rissa a Seal Point.

The brothers three . . . A trio of Himalayan males owned by Ann Peyton, Peyton Place Cattery, in Ventura, California. Left to right: Peyton Place Cugat, Peyton Place Little Joshua, and Peyton Place Kay-Si.

BREED RECOGNITION IN ACFA

The Executive Council of the ACFA voted 15 to 1 to accept the Himalayan as a new breed and to approve the Standard composed by the Ben Borretts of Canada. Carl Darnell was appointed to form the breed section for the Himalayan within ACFA.

CFA RECOGNIZES THE HIMALAYAN

In a letter to Mrs. Goforth dated December 18, 1957, from Mrs. Myrtle Shipe, at that time Secretary of the Cat

Fanciers Association, she was informed that "Himalayan cats were discussed in the Board meeting and I am very happy to advise you that they are to be recognized as pure bred cats and eligible for F. R. registration in CFA, after three generations have been registered by affidavit . . . Hope you are pleased with this action by the Board." Other cat associations followed suit, and now Himalayans are recognized by all of the American cat associations.

Triple Champion Mingchiu Mandella of Sahadi, photographed as a kitten by her breeder, Mrs. S. M. Harding of England, before her importation by the author in the mid-1960's. Mandella was *Cats Magazine* All Eastern Seal Point Himalayan Female for 1966.

Briarry Suzannah, bred by Mr. B. Stirling-Webb of England and owned by Mrs. S. M. Harding. She is the mother of Champion Mingchiu Monique and also mother of Triple U.S. Champion Mingchiu Nita, imported and owned by the author.

Mrs. Marguerita Goforth, pioneer in the breed, holding Ch. Goforth's Grand Design, Seal Point male born in August 1957. He was All Western and All American Himalayan in 1959 according to *Cats Magazine.* At her side is Princess Himalayan Hope, great, great granddam of the Himalayan line at her Goforth Cattery in California.

GOFORTH CATS SET THE PACE

Not only did Mrs. Goforth produce the first champion, but her Goforth's Grand Design became the first All American honors, in 1959. In succeeding years there were many other Goforth All American honors winners. In 1962 Goforth's Lassus Kandy and Goforth's Lodestar were Best and Best Opposite All American Himalayans. In 1964 her Quadruple Champion Goforth's P-Nut Kandy of Sabito was Best Opposite Sex Himalayan to the Borretts' Chestermere's Chen-Soo, who won All American title that year. The Borretts were leading breeders in Canada; their bloodlines, based exclusively on English import lines, won handsomely in both countries in the early days, as well as today!

Chapter 3

THE CREATION OF THE HIMALAYAN IN ENGLAND

The Colourpoint Longhair, as the Himalayan is called in Great Britain, was recoginzed by the Governing Council of the Cat Fancy in 1955. This recognition came as a direct result of many years of hard work and dedication by Mr. Brian Stirling-Webb at his Briarry Cattery in Richmond, England.

In Brian Vesey Fitzgerald's book *Cats*, a British publication, Mr. Fitzgerald states, "Brian Stirling-Webb of England, following the lines of Virginia Cobb's pre-war experiments, produced Sealpoints and Bluepoints, and the GCCF accepted these cats and called them Color Points." Over the years Mr. Stirling-Webb had corresponded with Virginia Cobb regarding her experimental breeding, and by the mid-1950's he had produced cats of such quality that recognition and championship status at the cat shows followed.

In England the cat was listed as a Colourpoint Longhair rather than a "new breed" so that breeding to Persians could continue to guarantee the Persian body type. In the United States the cat was considered a separate breed and named Himalayan in respect to the color pattern and because it was more "concise" than Seal Point Longhair Colorpoint.

In succeeding years Mr. Stirling-Webb was greatly aided in his breeding program by Mrs. S.M. Harding, owner of the Mingchiu Cattery in Surrey. She has also devoted a major portion of her time and knowledge to the breed and took in some of the cats from the Briarry Cattery upon the death of Mr. Stirling-Webb. Mrs. Harding's emphasis had been with the Chocolate and Lilac colors, though she has produced magnificent cats in all four colors over the years and has exported breeding pairs to many countries of the world to help establish the breed. Many catteries in the United States, including the author's, are founded on her lines. It was from Mr. Stirling-

Webb that the Ben Borretts of Canada purchased their original stock after a visit to his cattery several years ago.

EARLY BREEDINGS

During the early years of Mr. Stirling-Webb's breeding program it was necessary to keep introducing many self-colored cats, and other self-colored cats carrying the Siamese color pattern genes, along with the Persians. Early Briarry pedigrees show names like Ch. Baralan Boy Blue, Ch. Thiepval Enchantress, Ch. Thiepval Paragon and Kala Sabu. Later names became identified with colorpoint breeding, and we see Ch. Briarry Euan, which was a strong influence on the colorpoint program. Other names which appear behind not only English pedigrees but on those in the United States include Abu Hett, Valparago, Zoltan, Malachite and Eustace, to name a few of the males. The queens included Ch. Briarry Gohar, Bizbod, Larkspur, Euphemia, Roxana, Suzannah, Jehane and Candytuft, to name just a few with the Briarry prefix.

It is with these cats that the Briarry name came to fame, as well as the many others which shall have to remain unnamed now, all the products of Mr. Stirling-Webb's breeding program for so many years. Mr. Kirby-Smith and Mrs. Watts were also breeding Himalayans in these early days.

After their acceptance at the cat shows for championship status the cats gained wide attention. By 1958 Ch. Briarry Morenna, a beautiful Blue Point, captured the Best Longhaired Kitten in Show win at the Kensington Cat Club show. This important win was considered a significant breakthrough for the Colorpoints to attain top show wins.

Mrs. Harding was winning handsomely with her cats (now bearing the Mingchiu Cattery prefix) and she exported many of her fine kittens and adults to the United States. One of these was the magificent Quadruple Champion Mingchiu Tal, which helped establish Rose Levy's Harobed Cattery on Long Island. Another was the author's Ch. Mingchiu Mandarin of Sahadi, winner of 34 British awards by the time he was one year of age and the first Colorpoint to become (in 1965) an international champion on both sides of the Atlantic.

Mingchiu Mandarin photographed at four months of age. Mandarin was shown in England, Scotland and Wales before being imported by Joan Brearley into the United States, where he began his American championship. Mandarin is the only International Champion Himalayan in the history of the breed.

Other important Mingchiu cats behind Mrs. Harding's breeding were Ch. Mingchiu Polo, Shan, Sebastian (a Grand Champion) and many, many others, including the important Chocolates and Blue Points of which Mrs. Harding was so proud.

Today, more and more Himalayans are being seen — and are winning — at the British shows. Mrs. Harding is still among the top contenders, along with others represented photographically in this book. We see the names of Mrs. Doreen

Future International Champion Mingchiu Mandarin of Sahadi photographed at seven months of age by his breeder, Mrs. S. M. Harding of England.

Mingchiu Polo, Seal Point male photographed here by his breeder, Mrs. S. M. Harding of England, at seven months of age. Polo was a top show winner in England in the 1960's.

Hoyle and her Hardendale Colourpoints; Mrs. S.A. Hughes and her Sarobi name; Mrs. Bentinck's Copplestone line; and Mrs. M.E. Amphlett and her Denmaur Colourpoints. Many others have been captured by the beauty of the Himalayan and exhibit extensively and continue to work to improve the breed.

Their successes, however, are based on the years of breeding and experimentation of the remarkable Mr. Brian Stirling-Webb and Mrs. S.M. Harding, who contributed so much to the development of this magnificent cat.

THE BRITISH STANDARD
FOR
COLOURPOINT — LONG-HAIRS

COAT: Fur long, thick and soft in texture, frill full. Colour to be seal, blue or chocolate-pointed with appropriate body colour as for Siamese (i.e., cream, glacial white or ivory respectively). Points to be dense and body shading, if any, to be the same as the points.

HEAD: Broad and round with width between ears. Face and nose short. Ears small and tufted and cheeks well developed.

EYES: Shape: Large, round and full. Colour: Clear, bright and decidedly blue, the deeper the better.

BODY: Cobby and low on leg.

TAIL: Short and full, not tapering (a kink shall be considered a defect).

CONDITION: N.B. — Any similarity in *type* to Siamese to be considered most undesirable and incorrect.

Scale of Points

Coat	15
Point and Body Colour	10
Head	25
Shape of Eye	10
Colour of Eye	10
Body	10
Tail	10
Condition	10
Total	100

Chapter 4

HIMALAYANS IN OTHER COUNTRIES

THE BREED IN CANADA . . . Ben and Ann Borrett

Ben and Ann Borrett of Alberta, Canada quickly fell in love with the Himalayan cats. Fortunately, they also realized that there was much work to be done in the breed and weren't afraid to take it on. Their interest was deep, and they quickly set about trying to perfect the breed through careful planned breeding to establish both the correct Persian type and the glamorous Himalayan color pattern.

Perhaps the best example of this dedication toward perfection was their pride in having produced their magnificent Chestermere Kinuba. Kinuba was later sold to Boris Teron and Larry Keely in Chicago, Illinois in 1964. Under their campaigning Kinuba made history for the breed in this country by winning handsomely at the cat shows and by being the perfect example of what the Borretts proclaimed to be their ideal in the breed to date.

Kinuba was the first Himalayan to become a Grand Champion in four of the cat associations. Her complete cat show records can be found in our chapter on Top Cats elsewhere in this book.

Through the Borretts' interest in Siamese cats they became aware of the early experimental breedings being conducted with the Himalayan cat in mind. Their early imports were from the English Briarry bloodlines. The Borretts were asked to draw up a proposed Standard for the breed in 1957, and this Standard for the breed is virtually the same one used today in both their country and the U.S.

Their Chestermere Choi, a Seal Point female, was the first Himalayan ever to win a Best In Show. This win was under

Quintuple Champion Mingchiu Roli of Harobed, a Chocolate Point male imported and owned by Rose Levy of Long Island, New York.

judge Irene Powell in 1960. Their Chestermere Dumpling was the first Blue Point female to win a Best Cat Award in an all-breed show. Grand Champion Chestermere Chen-Soo was the first Himalayan to win four Bests In Show in one weekend . . . ! This was in 1965 in Winnipeg, Canada, and a feat Chen-Soo accomplished many times. His reputation as a Best In Show winner was well known and well respected.

Many of the Chestermere cats owned by other exhibitors

have set records and made championships and grand championships in both Canada and the United States, and continue to do so. The Chestermere prefix on any Himalayan means quality and cats with winning ways.

The Borretts' son, Bart, was born in 1964. Ben Borrett at one time was an international cattle judge. They owned the Chestermere cattle ranch and were active breeders until recently, when the cattle were sold. They kept the ranch when Ben retired in 1954 and devoted more and more of their time to their beloved Himalayan cats.

Himalayan owners and breeders owe a great debt to the Borretts, not only for their integrity in their own private breeding program but also for their active participation over the years in matters concerning the development of the breed all over the world. Their name and the name Chestermere are an integral part of the history of the breed.

International Champion Mingchiu Mandarin of Sahadi after completing his championships in England, Scotland and Wales, and before leaving for the United States. This magnificent Seal Point male was imported by Joan Brearley as a show cat and stud at her Sahadi Cattery in New York. Breeder was Mrs. S. M. Harding.

EARLY HIMALAYANS IN GERMANY

Almost at the same time the Himalayan was being developed in England and the United States, a similar breeding program was being pursued in Germany.

In the 1950's Frau Henrietta Schafer brought along an excellent line of Seal Point Himalayans which were known at the shows by her cattery name of Vogelsberg. By the 1960's the Robachsburg Cattery began working on the breed in earnest and Frau H. Romback began to introduce the Blue Point Himalayans. Her crosses and her foundation cat, Bubi von Sameck, founded her line, though Frau Schafer's Vogelsberg cats were also in the line.

Some of the other early German exhibitors of Himalayans were Ilse Gendermann, Elisaneth Kirsten, Georg Keferstein, Irmgard Florensky and Ferdinand Graef.

HIMALAYANS IN HOLLAND

A biologist named Miss van Wessem introduced the Himalayan to Holland in the early 1960's. Working with Siamese and Blue-eyed White Persians at her Siyah Gush Cattery at Gronsveld, Limburg, Holland, she finally came up with the desired combination which resulted in Himalayan cats! Blue Persian breedings later brought her the Blue and Lilac colorpoints to her line.

Siyah Gush Gazidan, whelped in June, 1961, was her first Himalayan Seal Point, and the first Chocolate Point, whelped July 24, 1961, was Siyah Gush Hela. Miss van Wessem is still active in the breeding of Himalayans, and Hela produced yet another litter of kittens to further the line at the age of eleven.

Opposite:
Mr. W. S. Steele, President of the Scottish Cat Club, bidding farewell to Scottish champion Mingchiu Mandarin of Sahadi. After completing his championships in England, Wales and Scotland, Mandarin was exported to Joan Brearley of New York where he made his American championship and became top stud at her Sahadi Cattery. Mandarin is the only International Champion in the breed; bred by Mrs. S. M. Harding of England.

Other Dutch catteries, of course, which breed Himalayan kittens have acquired their stock from English imports as well as crosses from important lines all over Europe. Holland's first Red Point was imported from America and was named White's Lilly. This queen was from Goforth breeding.

When White's Lilly was bred to International Champion Adonis von der Rombachsburg, the first kitten to be bred by this cattery in 1964, they produced a Tortie Point Himalayan which later became International Champion Viviane van Hoog-Moersbergen. Viviane later became the property of Mme. Coupleux and lived in Paris, France.

Tokyo, Japan: A television program about cat shows hosted by the Japan Cat Fanciers Association. At left are Baron and Mrs. Shirane, who are largely responsible for the popularity of cats in Japan. Next to Mrs. Shirane is Richard Gebhardt, guest American judge for the show, next to Mr. Gebhardt is Bess Higuchi, cat judge living in the U.S. and member of the C.F.A. International Committee. Extreme right is the host of the Japanese TV program.

Best Longhair Kittens Any Variety at the 1970 National Cat Show in London, England were Mrs. S. M. Harding's Mingchiu Squilla and Mingchiu Xanko.

By the early 1970's the Baroness v. Heerdt was exhibiting her Red Point male International Champion Unexpected Victory Van't Benthuys. By the beginning of the 1970's the French-born European cat show judge, Mevr. Prose-Imbert, was also working with Miss van Wessem on developing further the Chocolate and Lilac Point Himalayans.

It was plain to see that Himalayans were "catching hold" and that the various colorpoints were beginning to appear. Additionally, it is plain to see by the several International Championship titles that the breeders of this new breed were devoted to giving as much public exposure as possible to the Himalayan to assure its future in the European cat fancy.

39

EARLY HIMALAYANS IN FRANCE

An English import named Amska Blue Masque was the first to herald this breed in France. Imported by Mme. Gamichon in 1959 along with other English-bred queens, she was the beginning of the "true" Himalayan lines in France. Before these imports, France's Himalayans had been bred largely from Birmen cats, which did much harm to both breeds. This unfortunate experiment stopped upon the arrival of more and more of the pure-bred specimens from England.

HIMALAYANS IN SWITZERLAND AND SCANDINAVIA

Scandinavian Himalayans are descended from the English and Dutch lines. The same applies to the breed in Switzerland. Switzerland, because of its close proximity to Germany, where initial breedings were being conducted at almost the same time as they were in England, also contained German lines. The same holds true today, though the impact of the English lines is predominant in all countries abroad both then and now.

HIMALAYANS IN THE ORIENT

The Japanese people have always been known for their great love of cats. After World War II the cat fancy really blossomed in Japan, and many cats of many breeds were both imported and exported. But while the Japanese are working wonders with their Persian breeding, the introduction of Himalayan cats did not occur until very recently, and there is as yet no significant history of the Himalayan cat in Japan.

Chapter 5

THE BREED'S "TOP CATS"

In every breed of cat that has come along there has always been a succession of outstanding specimens which have helped bring the breed to public attention. Such was the case with the exotic new breed — the Himalayan.

When the breed first came to public attention in the mid-1950's, the first top cat to make a name for the breed and itself was Ch. Goforth's Prince Hopeful. This exquisite Seal Point male was whelped in July, 1955, bred by Marguerita Goforth. He was the first male Himalayan champion in the United States and was honored by being chosen to have his photograph appear on the 1958 sticker seals issued by the National Cat Week committee. His sire was Goforth's Sir Diamond and the queen was Goforth's Coquette, two important breeding cats at Mrs. Goforth's cattery in California. After his great success as the beautiful example of this exotic new breed, Prince lived out his life at Mrs. Robert Sugden's cattery in Yuma, Arizona. This fabulous cat did much in those early days to bring interest to breeding Himalayans on a grand scale.

Another of Mrs. Goforth's cats also came along to further popularize the Himalayan. Born in 1957, Ch. Goforth's Chocolate Soldier gained the distinction of being the first Chocolate Point Himalayan on record in the breed. In 1959 he won the *Cats Magazine* All Western Chocolate Point Himalayan award and helped establish the Himalayan as a winning breed at the shows.

On the distaff side was Ch. Goforth's Winsome Lass of Dao. Lass was a litter sister to the famous Prince Hopeful. She was also the second Himalayan female to win championship status. Lass was bred by Mrs. Goforth and later sold to Don Yoder of Kansas City.

The magnificent Quintuple Ch. Mingchiu Tal of Harobed, imported from England by Rose Levy of Plainview, Long Island. Winner of many *Cats Magazine* awards, Tal was truly a magnificent Blue Point Himalayan.

By the early 1960's the breed was causing quite a stir among some interested fanciers on the East Coast. Most prominent and dedicated of these was Rose Levy, owner of the Harobed Cattery in Plainview, Long Island, New York. Mrs. Levy imported her cats from Mrs. S. M. Harding, owner of the Mingchiu Cattery in Surry, England. Her cattery was based on the Briarry lines, which created the breed in that country.

Rose Levy's Champion Mingchiu Tal of Harobed, a magnificent Blue Point male, was the main attraction in the breed in the East for many years, throughout his impressive show career. In 1964 Tal was the winner of the Best Blue Point Male

Himalayan Award from *Cats Magazine*, and was a champion in many of the associations. His show winning record and awards were numerous and his personality a tribute to the breed. But tragedy struck at the peak of his career. Rose Levy's cattery was broken into and Tal was stolen . . .There was never a trace of Tal again, and the mysterious circumstances of his disappearance left a pall that touched all who had come to know and admire this marvelous cat. Fortunately, in spite of this terrible blow, Rose Levy continued to import and to breed and to win with cats that came to be known by her Harobed prefix and their great quality.

Rose Levy imported Mingchiu Pearlas as a breeding queen. Her show career was equally impressive when compared with Tal's and continued until Pearlas was almost ten years of age. A big winner and a good show queen, Pearlas still enjoys her old age at Mrs. Levy's cattery and is still in beautiful condition and coat.

Jane Levy with her daughter Nancy and one of her mother's Blue Point Himalayan show cats, Double Grand Champion and Sextuple Champion Mingchiu Pearlas of Harobed.

Grand Champion Hima Tab Pago, Blue Point male, sired by Gr. Ch.
Chestermere Chi Chi of Hima Tab *ex* Ch. Hima Tab Lil' Bo Peep. Pago
was the first Himalayan to make a CFA Grand Championship, and at
just eight months of age. He has many Best Kitten in Show awards to
his credit. Owned by Mrs. LaVerne Grusell of Ashland, Ohio.

Mrs. Levy has continued to import from Mrs. Harding to
supplement her breeding stock and is now breeding and
showing Himalayans of quality in all the beautiful colors. Her
cats have been sought out for use in advertising photographs.

In February, 1965 the author imported Mingchiu Mandarin
from Mrs. S. M. Harding in England. Other Himalayans which
she imported earlier had prompted her to import a stud to
establish her line of Himalayans at her Sahadi Cattery. She
wrote to Mrs. Harding and expressed this desire, and an arrangement was made whereby the first top Seal Point would
first be finished in England and then sent to America to serve

here. The cat was Mandarin, whelped on March 13, 1964. His progress was carefully watched by Mrs. Harding, and in January and February of 1965 Mrs. Harding felt he was ready to win. During those two months he completed championships in England, Scotland and Wales and was featured, along with the story of his exportation to the U.S., on the cover of the May issue of England's *Our Cats* magazine.

The very next weekend after his British successes, Mandarin made his championship in the United States and became the first Himalayan in the history of the breed to have gained championship in both countries. Mandarin was the first Himalayan champion on both sides of the Atlantic. Mandarin, sired by Briarry Valparago *ex* Briarry Roxanna, was a potent and persistent stud and was used carefully in American breeding programs. Mandarin used to perch on a ceiling rafter in the living room and when a queen in season walked by he would silently pounce down on her and have her bred before she ever knew what had happened or where he had come from. These matings were referred to as Mandarin's "flights of fancy," and those who witnessed this act used to marvel at the way he sat sphinx-like for hours with nothing moving but his eyes as the females passed by beneath him unaware of what lurked above. As he approached his old age he was less athletic but equally gentle. A gentleman always, and a great companion to humans, he was more than worthy of the dedication of this book by his admiring owner.

The top-winning Himalayan in the breed is Quadruple Champion Chestermere Kinuba. Kinuba was the first Himalayan to make his Grand Championship in four cat associations. He was the first Cat Fanciers Association Best in Show winner as well. This wonderful Blue Point male was born on January 10, 1962 at the Ben Borretts' cattery in Canada. When he died on March 7, 1969 as a result of a nephritic condition discovered shortly after his sixth birthday, he had racked up an enviable show record that will not be equalled in the near future.

When he retired from the show ring in 1968 his awards included: All American Blue Point Himalayan for 1962-1963; All American Honorable Mention Blue Point Himalayan for 1963-1964; All Midwestern Blue Point Himalayan 1964. He

Grand Champion Chestermere Kinuba of Nevah-Tep. This sensational
Blue Point male was born January 10, 1962, and died March 7, 1969,
after a fantastic show ring career which included many Best Cat in
Show awards. Owned by Larry Keely and Boris Teron of Chicago,
Illinois. Kinuba was the first Himalayan to win a CFA Best Cat in Show
award and was the first Himalayan Grand Champion in no less than
four cat fancy associations, and first Himalayan Royal Merit Quadruple Grand Champion in the ACFA. Bred by Mr. and Mrs. Ben Borrett
of Canada.

International Champion Mingchiu Mandarin featured on the cover of
the May, 1965 issue of *Our Cats* magazine, published in England, and
announcing his exportation to Joan Brearley in the United States. He
is being held by Mr. W. S. Steele, President of the Scottish Cat Club
after completing his Scottish championship. He is also a champion in
England and Wales, and later in the United States. Breeder was Mrs.
S. M. Harding, England.

Our Cats

AUTHORITATIVE   THE·WORLD·OF·CAT   ENTERTAINING

INSTRUCTIVE   SPANS·CAT·LOVERS·   COMPREHENSIVE

Mr. W. S. Steele, President of the Scottish Cat Club, with
CHAMPION MINGCHIU MANDARIN, a Colourpoint of
outstanding quality bred by Mrs. S. M. Harding. Mandarin is now owned by Mrs. Brearley, of Eaglewood, New
Jersey, U.S.A. A feature in this issue will tell you more
about him and the breed he so worthily represents.

MAY 1965

2/6

won the Purina Award for Highest Scoring American Himalayan for 1964-1965 and won again the following year. He won the CFA All Star Award for 1965-1966 as Best Himalayan. Kinuba was All American and Highest Scoring American Himalayan 1965 through 1967 and #1 Longhair Male according to *Cats Magazine's* May, 1967 issue. He was also #4 Longhair Male and Best Himalayan in CFA for 1966-1967. In the 1967 show season he was #2 cat as best Longhair Male in ACFA and CFA's #2 cat that year as well.

Grand Champion Quiksilver Cascade. Top Himalayan in the Nation the year she was shown. This magnificent Blue Point Himalayan female, bred and owned by Will Thompson of Burbank, California, was a daughter of Grand Champion Chestermere Chahila.

Quadruple Champion Harobed Iris, born May 12, 1967, and bred and owned by Rose Levy of Plainview, Long Island, New York. Iris, an outstanding Tortie Point Himalayan was *Cats Magazine* All Eastern Tortie Point Himalayan in both 1968 and 1971. Iris has won in the finals at many shows with Second and Fifth Best Cat awards.

Kinuba also left his mark on the breed as a stud cat with many champion and grand champion offspring . . . a record owners Boris Teron and Larry Keely can be proud of as they carry on with his get under their Nevah-Tep Cattery prefix.

One of these outstanding cats was Grand Ch. Nevah-Tep's Vogue. Born in March, 1970, this gorgeous Seal Point was CFA's Highest Scoring Himalayan in the 1971-1972 show season and won Best Cat in the International Himalayan Society and in The Himalayan Society in 1972. Other outstanding Himalayans bear the Nevah-Tep name as well.

While these cats in no way represent *all* of the winners and pace setters for the breed over the years, it can be said that they were prominent in the breed and attracted many fanciers to the Himalayan. And it is obvious their numbers were legion, since few breeds have gained such a fast rise in popularity as our Himalayan. We are sure that the future is bright for the Himalayans as they continue to gain fans all over the world. Careful breeding has continued to show improvement in the conformation and coloration, and we can now boast that we are "holding our own" against even the most superb of the Persians!

Peyton Place Kay-Si, Seal Point male bred and owned by Ann Peyton of Ventura, California. Kay-Si was sired by Kim-Mari Kava *ex* Peyton Place Sindchez. Kay-Si has twice been Best Himalayan Kitten over 19 other Himalayans and was Third Best Longhair Kitten twice under judges Cathy Hummer and David Mare.

Chapter 6
THE HIMALAYAN AS A BREED

THE HIMALAYAN STANDARD

POINT SCORE

Head (Including size and shape of eyes, ear shape and set)...30
Type (Including shape, size, bone, and length of tail) 20
Coat 10
Condition 10
Body Color 10
Point Color 10
Eye Color 10

HEAD: Round and massive, with great breadth of skull. Round face with round underlying bone structure. Well set on a short, thick neck.

NOSE: Short, snub and broad. With "Break."

CHEEKS: Full.

JAWS: Broad and powerful.

CHIN: Full and well-developed.

EARS: Small, round tipped, tilted forward, and not unduly open at base. Set far apart, and low on the head fitting into (without distorting) the rounded contour of the head.

EYES: Large, round and full. Set far apart and brilliant, giving a sweet expression to the face.

BODY: Of cobby type — low on the legs, deep in the chest, equally massive across shoulders and rump, with a short well-rounded middle piece. Large or medium in size. Quality the determining consideration rather than size.

BACK: Level.

LEGS: Short, thick and strong. Forelegs straight.

PAWS: Large, round and firm. Toes carried close, five in front and four behind.

TAIL: Short, but in proportion to body length. Carried without a curve and at an angle lower than the back.

COAT: Long and thick, standing off from the body. Of fine texture, glossy and full of life. Long all over the body, including the shoulders. The ruff immense and continuing in a deep frill between the front legs. Ear and Toe tufts long. Brush very full.

WITHHOLD AWARDS: Locket or button. Kinked or abnormal tail. Crossed eyes. Incorrect number of toes. White toes.

COLOR: Body: Even, with subtle shading when allowed. Allowance to be made for darker coloring on older cats. Shading should be subtle with definite contrast between points. *Points:* Mask, ears, legs, feet, tail dense and clearly defined. All of the same shade. Mask covers entire face including whisker pads and is connected to ears by tracings. Mask should not extend over top of head. No ticking or white hairs in points.

HIMALAYAN COLORS

SEAL POINT: Body even pale fawn to cream, warm in tone, shading gradually into lighter color on the stomach and chest. Points deep seal brown. *Nose Leather:* Same color as points. *Paw Pads:* Same color as points. *Eye Color:* Deep vivid blue.

CHOCOLATE POINT: Body ivory with no shading. Points milk-chocolate color, warm in tone. *Nose Leather:* Cinnamon Pink. *Paw Pads:* Cinnamon Pink. *Eye Color:* Deep vivid blue.

BLUE POINT: Body bluish white, cold in tone, shading gradually to white on stomach and chest. Points blue. *Nose Leather:* Slate colored. *Paw Pads:* Slate colored. *Eye Color:* Deep vivid blue.

LILAC POINT: Body glacial white with no shading. Points frosty grey with pinkish tone. *Nose Leather:* Lavender Pink. *Paw Pads:* Lavender Pink. *Eye Color:* Deep vivid blue.

FLAME POINT: Body creamy white. Points delicate orange flame, free of barring and uniform in color. *Nose Leather:* Same color as points. *Paw Pads:* Same color as points. *Eye Color:* Deep vivid blue.

Grand Champion Kits Precious, Blue Cream Point born May 22, 1972; bred and owned by Elmer G. and Ruth Kitsmiller of Simi Valley, California. In 1972 Precious was *Cats Magazine* Second Best All Western Tortie Point (before Blue Creams were color recognized) and Second Best All American Tortie Point. Both the International Himalayan Society and the Himalayan Society voted her Best Blue Cream Point in the Nation. In 1973 she was *Cats Magazine* Third Best All Western Tortie Point and in 1974 *Cats Magazine* Best All Western Blue Cream Point Himalayan and Second Best All American Blue Cream Point. She was also CFA's Second Best Himalayan in the Southwest Region and AHC Best Cat Western Region.

53

TORTIE POINT: Body creamy white. Points black with unbrindled patches of red and cream. *Eye Color:* Deep vivid blue.

BLUE CREAM POINT: Body bluish white or creamy white, shading gradually to white on the stomach and chest. Points blue with patches of cream. *Nose Leather:* Slate blue, pink, or a combination of slate blue and pink. *Paw Pads:* Slate blue, pink, or a combination of slate blue and pink. *Eye Color:* Deep vivid blue.

HOW THE BREED GOT ITS NAME

In Europe, the earliest breedings of the Siamese/Persian combinations were referred to as Colorpoints. Later, they were known on the continent as Khmers. This name held until 1955, when the breed was recognized by the Governing Council of the Cat Fancy in England, which established the name of Colourpoint Longhairs. (Note the English spelling of Colorpoint.) Following the British decision, the Continental countries also adopted the same name for purposes of unifying the breed in all countries.

In the beginning in the United States they were also called Colorpoints. It was Marguerite Goforth in the 1950's who gave the breed the tentative title of Himalayans, naming them after the color pattern found on Himalayan goats, rabbits and other animals. The name was voted on and approved, becoming "official" at the Board Meeting of the ACFA in December, 1957.

HIMALAYAN COAT CHARACTERISTICS

Himalayans have come a long way since their inception, and one of the most outstanding improvements has been in the fascinating coat characteristics and coloring! Today's Himalayan can equal the best Persians in the length and density of their coats, and it is a great achievement on the part of the dedicated breeders who have worked so hard on perfecting it!

However, along with the long hair come the same problems which have always gone along with the Persian-type coat. In

Kelly-Ko's Charlie strikes an impressive pose for the camera. This beautiful Seal Point male is owned by Pat Kelly, Kelly-Ko Cattery, Pine Bush, New York.

the grooming chapter we discuss the shedding seasons which must be endured with this breed, and there are other factors regarding the Himalayan coat which must be reckoned with; they are important to know.

FACTORS WHICH AFFECT COLOR

There are many factors which will influence the color of your Himalayan. I do not refer to Seal Point, Blue Point, etc. I refer to the shades within each Colorpoint. Let us use the Seal Point as an example, since it is the darkest of the colors and the variations of the Seal Points are the most noticeable.

Grand Champion Hima Tab Miss Muffet, a lovely Blue Point female, was the fourth female Himalayan to make a CFA Grand Championship and the first Himalayan kitten to consistently make the kitten finals during her ring career. During six shows (24 rings) she was in the finals 14 times; this included Best Kitten five times and Second Best Kitten nine times. This was at the time when there were only Best, Second Best and Best Opposite Kitten. She is also the dam of Gr. Ch. Hima Tab Dixie. Bred and owned by Mrs. LaVerne Grusell of Ashland, Ohio.

Grand Champion Kits Peaches 'N Cream, Tortie Point Himalayan, born April 16, 1970, bred and owned by Elmer and Ruth Kitsmiller of Simi Valley, California. In 1971 Peaches was *Cats Magazine* Third Best All Western and International Himalayan Society Best Tortie Point in the Nation.

Weather Conditions

In Himalayans — as in Siamese — exposure to extreme cold or heat will usually alter the color. Cold has a tendency to darken the seal coloring as well as the body coloring. Himalayans that shed in "clumps" rather than evenly all over will sometimes look spotted when the new hair appears and is darker in color.

Age

Age also is a factor. Without exception older cats will carry a darker coat than kittens in full bloom or cats which have come into their first few adult coats. With progressing age white hairs may also appear in the points as the points, and especially the mask, take on a grayish appearance.

Showing or Breeding

It is up to you to decide right away whether you wish to use your Himalayan male as a stud or as a show cat. You cannot successfully do both! Not with this color pattern.

Stud service darkens the body coat, so the more your cat is used at stud the darker the body coat will become, and you lose the beautiful color contrast between the points and body color.

If your Himalayan is an excellent specimen and worthy of a championship, it is wise to show the cat while it is young and in good coat. Then retire him at stud at the end of his successful show career. His wins will increase his desirability as a stud, and you will no longer have to worry about the contrast of color in the coat.

With females almost the same situation applies. Motherhood tends to darken the body coat. The same would hold true here. It would be wise to show a female to a championship, then retire her for motherhood.

English and American Ch. Mingchiu Tal of Harobed, a Blue Point male, photographed in November, 1963 at eight months of age. Tal was imported by Mrs. Rose Levy of Long Island, New York and made several U.S. championships starting in January, 1964. Bred by Mrs. S. M. Harding, England.

Effects of Food and Water on Body Color

Just as we know that a sick Himalayan will usually show "brindley" markings or "ticked" hair in the points, we can sometimes see the evidences of food and water affecting the coat.

Purified or highly chlorinated water compared to well water can make a marked difference in the color of body coat. Severe changes in diet, too much of a single food, excessive vitamins or medications, etc., all may take effect on the color. Any of these things may ruin an entire show season before they are corrected — so feed well and watch the water!

Playtime at Tomany Cattery! Eight-week-old kittens bred and owned by Mary Van Liew, Tomany Cattery, Kew Gardens, Long Island, New York.

HIMALAYAN TEMPERAMENT: The Perfect Choice!

For cat lovers who favor the appearance of the Siamese cat but can't tolerate their active life style or the raucous calling when they are in season, the Himalayan has to be considered the perfect alternative! For as we have stated before, the only likeness between the Siamese and the Himalayan is the color pattern.

The Himalayan is physically constructed like the Persian cat and carries the same passive, quiet, and affectionate personality as the other longhaired breeds in the Persian family . . . truly a cat that fits in with all life styles.

Just how well their behavior fits in with your family life can depend largely on how well you introduce it to its new surroundings, so a little extra care at the time you bring the kitten into the home will reap rewards from then on. The kitten or cat that is given affection will return it and will enjoy being handled and admired by all members of the family.

The independence the cat is known to possess is to be respected rather than criticized. But no matter what degree of independence your cat possesses, you will find that the cat will prefer being with the family, observing all that is going on. All cats are independent at times in varying degrees; it is a part of their character, so we might as well accept it as part of being a cat!

CHILDREN AND CATS

It is wise to teach children in the family how to pick up and hold a cat. A lot of scratches and struggles can be avoided if being picked up is not necessarily made to be a painful experience for the cat. The children should be told that a cat or kitten is picked up with two hands, one hand under the front legs and the other hand under the rear end, supporting the hind quarters. It should also be pointed out that although a cat flicks its tail around in the air in any number of ways and positions, it can be painful if bent or tucked under it in an unnatural way, and pressure or force on the tail should be avoided when in contact.

Children should also be taught to handle the cat gently and to keep it away from their faces even when the claws are cut. Cats can become frightened and panic and contact with the face can be dangerous at this time.

International Champion Mingchiu Mandarin and Triple Champion Mingchiu Mandella pose for a British automobile advertisement. Owned by Joan Brearley of New York, these Seal Point Himalayans have appeared in many magazine advertisements. Along with their show careers, they were much in demand for both magazine and television modeling appearances.

THE PROPER INTRODUCTION

The temperament of the Himalayan is such that it welcomes any and all additions to its family life. You will find that if you buy your kitten as the first pet in the family it will still welcome another cat or any other pet into its life. You will also find that it will adjust just as easily if it is the newest member of the family in which there are already other cats or dogs in residence.

The secret of having animals get along well together lies largely in making the proper introductions. Two animals that are simply put down in a room together will normally assume a "stand-off" attitude and may stalk each other; the meeting can go well or badly. But when they are kept within sight of one another, but with a screen or cage as a "divider" for a day or two, you will find they get on with one another right from that time on. They do not like to have to take a stand or establish "Territorial rights" upon meeting. But if they are allowed to view each other from neutral territory and see that both are invited and welcome within the family, they will assume the proper attitude.

The author is a great advocate of having two — not just one — pet of any kind. And the ideal situation is provided by buying them both at the same time. They are security for one another and company for each other when the family members are busy outside the house pursuing their other interests. People that go out to work all day or spend weekends away from home should have two cats, for these reasons especially. It will in no way deter the affection they will give the family, and it will also save the "wear and tear" on one cat if there are several children in the family!

Chapter 7

FEEDING AND NUTRITION

There are almost as many theories on feeding cats and kittens as there are breeders! Even the veterinarians are prescribing various diets for cats which may differ considerably from the advertisements we read in magazines and see on television. With so many commercial foods on the market these days, properly feeding our animals can become confusing! With the wide variety we are almost creating a generation of finicky eaters as we try by process of elimination to concoct the combinations our cats like best.

Everyone is agreed, however, that all the available cat chows are good. These chows, and water, are said to be all that is really required to maintain a healthy cat. We know this to be true when we read the list of ingredients featured on each package. The chow contains everything needed to provide a balanced diet, and in an even more digestible form than by fresh foods. However, there are cats and kittens that cannot enjoy or tolerate the chow diet; they must be fed regular foods or special diet rations prescribed by veterinarians.

Some veterinarians recommend raw or cooked meat, whereas others insist on including cereals and/or vegetables. The biggest controversy is over including milk in the diet. Some say milk is good for kittens but not for adult cats. Others say milk is good at any age for cats or kittens. My cats have enjoyed milk or even cream or ice cream throughout their lives.

The second largest controversy is over the feeding of fish. Contrary to story book tales that the favorite food of cats is fish, it is now proved that fish can be highly detrimental to a cat's health. While some cats may always have complete tolerance for it, others may prove to be allergic to fish. Other cats may have more serious complications, especially if it is served to them raw.

One of Rose Levy's magnificent Tortie Point Himalayans. Mrs. Levy is owner of the Harobed Cattery, Plainview, Long Island, New York. Photo by B.J. Studios.

CFA Ch. Hima-Shell Creme de Cocoa, Tortie Point. Her first time shown as an adult, this cat won the Best Himalayan rosette in the CFA show "Roses for Felines." Owned by Michelle Woods, Palos Hills, Illinois.

The basic explanation for this problem is said to be that the thiaminase enzyme in fish destroys the necessary thiamine in their diets, even though cooking the fish partially destroys the thiaminase enzyme. So if your cat craves fish, or has already developed a taste for it, serve it as a treat only and on rare occasions in cooked form!

TO EACH HIS OWN

After years of research and personal experience with cats, pretty much everyone is agreed that cat owners will eventually develop a favorite diet for their cats. Generally speaking, there are a few basic rules which should be observed to keep the diet well balanced. Keep this handy list available in your kitchen or cattery as a daily reminder:

* Always have your cat's favorite chow available 24 hours a day.
* Always have fresh water available, preferably in more than one place in the house.
* Feed vegetables, especially tomatoes, if they like them, to vary the diet and keep appetites at a peak.
* Feed fresh, good quality meat, slightly cooked or raw, as they prefer. Feed beef, lamb, veal, heart, kidney, liver and horsemeat once in a while.
* Add a vitamin supplement if desired and in quantity prescribed according to age and weight — or on veterinary advice.
* Feed once a day if dry cat chow is always available; feed twice a day if cat chow is not available.

Champion Goforth's Prince Hopeful, Seal Point male photographed at three years of age. It was Prince Hopeful that first got author Joan Brearley interested in Himalayans; his owner, Mrs. J. F. Goforth of San Diego, California, is largely responsible for the popularity of the breed in the United States.

Copplestone Maria, sired by Ch. Chestermere Copplestone *ex* Ch. X.O.X. Betula. Bred and owned by Mrs. I. Bentinck of Berkshire, England.

←

Ch. Kelly-Ko's Sundance, nine-month-old Flame Point male owned by Patricia Kelly of Pine Bush, New York. Mrs. Kelly is the owner of the Kelly-Ko Cattery.

FEEDING KITTENS

Kittens should be fed four times a day. An ideal schedule is as follows:

3- 6 months . . . 4 times a day
6- 9 months . . . 3 meals a day
9-12 months . . . 2 meals a day
1 year on . . . . 1 meal a day plus dry chow

Peyton Place Little Joshua, born in July, 1974. This lovely Blue Point Himalayan was sired by Kim-Mari Kava *ex* Peyton Place Sindchez; bred and owned by Ann Peyton of Ventura, California. Joshua won Fifth Best Kitten over 49 Longhairs at the 1974 Lancaster Show under judge Will Thompson.

GRASS

It is particularly unpleasant to some owners to see their cats eat grass and then promptly throw it up. Why do cats eat grass? Mostly it is to help them get rid of hairballs or other debris which might get into their stomachs, but is is also a way of getting rid of food which may not agree with them or may be spoiled and unfit to eat. At times eating grass has a laxative effect which your cat will realize instinctively even before you do.

The eating of grass should be left entirely up to the cat and the conscience of the owner, since eating grass is neither healthful nor harmful to the cat. Country cats have grass available to

Royal Merit Champion Robrick Woodsprite photographed at eight months of age. This Blue Point female is owned and bred by the Paul A. Buells of Mission, B.C., Canada.

Cat Lore Robespierre, a Seal Point male photographed at eight months of age. Bred by Laurie Stevens and Helen Arnold; the owner is co-breeder Laurie Stevens, Cat Lore Cattery, Chicago, Illinois.

Opposite:
Copplestone Maria, photographed as a kitten in the garden of Mrs. I. Bentinck's cattery in Berkshire, England. Sire was Ch. Chestermere Copplestone *ex* X.O.X. Betula.

them at all times and are more apt to develop the habit of eating grass for various reasons. Some apartment owners who know their cats enjoy grass grow it on their terraces or in flower pots in the cities.

CATNIP

Many cat owners also make catnip available to their pets. Some even grow their own catnip bushes among the shrubbery around the house or cattery, though it is available in pet shops everywhere. Fresh catnip can be a nice treat for your cat and is said to serve as a tonic. Cats' amusing behavior while "under the influence" can be charming and brings no harm to them. When buying catnip, just make sure to get it freshly packaged and to read the instructions on the box.

BONES

Do not give your animals meat bones of any kind, size or shape! There are treated synthetic bones which do not break or chip which are the only safe ones to provide.

TEETHING

Kittens usually get their first set of teeth at around four weeks. By six weeks they have a full set of "baby teeth" which usually lasts them until they fall out and are replaced by a permanent set between five and seven months.

Teeth are usually no problem, but the owner of a cat should be sure that none of them become infected or grow in crooked to ruin the bite or damage the rest of the teeth. Removing teeth is a matter for the veterinarian, and the most important thing the owner can do to insure good teeth is to feed a proper diet. The rest the cat itself can usually take care of. Dry foods will help keep the teeth clean. Also, artificial bones will help keep the teeth free from tartar.

If excess tartar does accumulate on the teeth, your veterinarian can scrape it off and make the rec mmended adjustment in the diet.

Chapter 8

GROOMING
YOUR HIMALAYAN

All longhaired cats require frequent grooming, and the Himalayan is no exception. Just as Persians tend to mat, so do the Himalayans. It is wise to get your cat used to being groomed while it, is still a kitten, since few cats have the patience to stand and be groomed for any length of time. If your cat is to be a show cat, it must be groomed and bathed on a regular basis, so it is wise to establish "ground rules" while the cat is still young.

TROUBLE SPOTS

If at all possible, get the kitten used to being on its back so that the stomach may be groomed and tangles that form under the front legs and between the back legs can be groomed with a minimum amount of struggle. Needless to say, extreme care should be taken when grooming in these areas. The flash of a steel comb near a cat's eyes or passing over testicles can be enough to make the cat nervous . . . one wrong move on your part and you are liable to be bitten or scratched — and with good reason! Such actions are likely to set the cat against grooming for the rest of its life, and it is difficult enough to keep the cat patient long enough to complete the job even under the *best* of conditions.

KITTEN COATS

A proper kitten coat can be in full bloom when the cat is about eight months of age. In the Himalayan the contrast between points and body color is strikingly beautiful: with proper grooming, many wins can be made in the show ring with this full coat. However, it is also around this age that cats begin to shed kitten coat and get into their adult coat, and you will begin to notice mats.

Grand Champion Miss Sue of Kelly-Ko, five-year-old Tortie Point female Himalayan, owned by Patricia Kelly, Kelly-Ko Cattery, Pine Bush, New York.

Opposite, top:
Nine-week-old Hima-Shell Taster Choice, Seal Point kitten owned and bred by Michelle Woods, Hima-Shell Cattery, Palos Hills, Illinois.

←
The magnificent and top-winning Flame Point Himalayan Double Champion Harobed Mandrangoro, born in June, 1972, and sired by Grand Champion and Quadruple Champion Harobed Red Baron *ex* Quadruple Ch. Harobed Kaleidoscope. In 1973 and 1974 Manny was *Cats Magazine* All Eastern and All American Flame Point Himalayan and in 1974 was All American Male Himalayan. In just eight shows between April and October of 1973, Manny won one Best Cat in Show, one Second Best Cat in Show, six Thirds, five Fourths and two Fifth Bests in Show! This fantastic homebred is owned and shown by Rose Levy, Harobed Cattery, Plainview, Long Island, New York.

Ch. Hima Tab Michelle, a Seal Point granddaughter of Gr. Ch. Hima Tab Dixie. Owned by Mrs. LaVerne Grusell of Ashland, Ohio.

MATTING

Matting is the scourge of the show cat owner. Some Himalayans, just like some Persians, have a "cottony" coat. This cottony coat mats even more quickly and thickly than the normal longhair coat and takes the form of "plates" or "felt pads." These are sometimes impossible to comb out and must be cut off, which means the end of a show coat for another season. However, the normal mats may be eliminated by patient combing and brushing.

The proper way to eliminate mats is to start combing them out from the bottom and in toward the skin. Try separating them by pulling them apart with your fingers and then combing each section out one at a time. If the mat is too thick to get the comb through, try slitting it with   scissors to start. Using the scissors from the body outward, cut down the length of the hair to separate the mat and then try combing again.

If the procedure doesn't seem to work, try one of the detangling preparations on sale at pet stores, or pay a professional groomer to show you how it is done. If your cat is very restless, perhaps you are being too rough or are pulling the hair too hard. There is a knack to grooming, so don't you lose patience either!

Ch. Hima Tab Seventh Heaven, Blue Point female owned by Mrs. LaVerne Grusell of Ashland, Ohio. The sire was Gr. Ch. Hima Tab Pago *ex* Gr. Ch. Hima Tab Miss Muffet.

top left:
Royal Merit Robrick K'San, owned by Mary Robinson and bred by the Paul Buells of Canada.

top right:
Hima Tab Mr. Somebody pictured at six and one-half weeks of age. This most promising kitten was tragically lost because of an allergy to Vitamin D. Bred and mourned by Mrs. LaVerne Grusell of the Hima Tab Cattery, Ashland, Ohio.

Ch. Chestermere Copplestone perched on a shelf in the outdoor cattery with his son Australian Ch. Copplestone Bonner and a daughter, Copplestone Marisa, now also in Australia. Bred by Mrs. I. Bentinck, Berkshire, England.

Flame Point male, Dragonseed Kumquat, owned by Elaine Marsh of Oceanside, New York, and photographed by Pat Horton.

Purring Lane's Snow Poppy, top Flame Point female that won 14 finals awards in five shows. Owned by the Purring Lane Cattery.

SHEDDING

Mats are usually the result of not enough grooming to remove the dead hairs that form into mats. Try to anticipate the shedding season for your cat — especially if it is to be a show cat. As you notice more and more hair staying behind in the brush, consider the season; if it is spring or fall, increase the grooming schedule so that you groom twice as often or whenever necessary to prevent mats. The constant grooming will not only prevent mats and help remove dead hair but also will encourage the growth of the new hair and keep the coat evenly distributed all over the body.

NORMAL GROOMING REQUIREMENTS

I must emphasize the importance of grooming on a regular basis once again. A light brushing with a "once over lightly" with a comb can keep any longhaired cat in good condition and prevent matting. Time put out for this regular grooming, you will find, is time well spent.

BATHING THE CAT

It is true that cats keep themselves clean. They are naturally clean animals, and it will seldom if ever be necessary to give your cat a bath . . . barring some accident such as an encounter with a skunk (requiring a bath with tomato juice) or having something spilled on it or perhaps a barn cat that is to become a house cat, etc.

But if your cat is a show cat, baths will be necessary, and you should start the bathing when the cat is very young.

Bathing a cat can be a harrowing experience for both the cat and the owner, especially if the cat is a water-hater. Contrary to popular opinion, some cats like water, but even those that do not panic at water may not like a bath with all its soapings and drying processes. The cat may put up quite a struggle if it is not used to a bath or if it is not bathed properly.

No cat should be bathed too frequently, or all the natural oils will be removed from the coat. Today's show cats, with show

Saykiala Pipaluk, photographed at three-and-a-half weeks of age at Mrs. J. Dayton Saykiala's Cattery in Essex, England.

ring appearances nearly every weekend, are frequently bathed on a weekly basis; care must be taken to see that oil is put back into their coats with the proper shampoos and rinses. Consult with your pet shop owner as to his selection of both shampoo and rinse and read all instructions carefully — *before* starting the bath! Also get all your grooming tools, the dryer and the towels handy. Once you have waterproofed yourself you are ready to start!

Be sure there is a rubber mat at the bottom of the sink so that the cat can feel secure about its footing. Start the bath by having warm water half way up the sink and try to submerge the cat gently by adding warm water gradually to the water already in the sink. Do not, of course, try to submerge the head . . . and wash that last. For the face, first use a wet face-cloth with a little shampoo on it and then wipe off with a well-rinsed

Triple Champion Red Sunset, a Flame Point Himalayan who likes to shake hands. Among mammals, cats rate very high in intelligence and can easily be taught tricks. Photo by Dr. Herbert R. Axelrod.

Kit's Bo Peep, seven-month-old Tortie Point Himalayan owned by Ruth Kitsmiller, Simi Valley, California.

Three-month-old male Seal Point owned by Ruth Kitsmiller of Simi Valley, California.

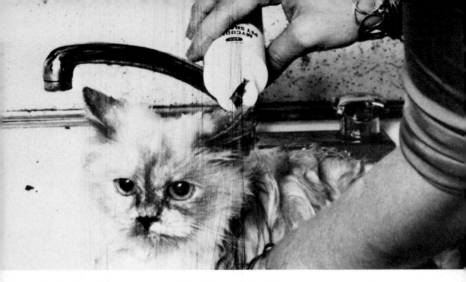

Using a shampoo specifically created for cats, pour shampoo over entire length of body. Start at back of the neck, then go down the back and tail and the four feet. Save the head until last.

face cloth. A soft silent spray attachment on the faucet will greatly aid in rinsing and wetting the cat before and after you apply the shampoo. Usually one soaping will be sufficient, but a good rinsing is essential to remove every last vestige of soap from the coat.

Be warming up the dryer a safe distance away, and remove the cat from the sink to the grooming table in a big Turkish towel. Do not *rub* dry! *Pat* dry and wipe down. If you rub dry with a towel you will add tangles and mats to the hair. While the dryer is warming and the cat is getting used to the sound of it — certainly not for the first time! — get it used to the feel of the soft brush you will be using. Gently go over the entire cat with the brush, wiping off the excess water with a corner of the towel. Then, with the dryer and starting at the back end of the cat, on the side of the body, and keeping the direct stream of air away from the face, begin the drying process. Hold the dryer several inches away from the body and try to dry evenly all over the body.

When washing the cat's stomach and working lather into coat all over the body, hold the cat by grasping its front paws between your thumb and fingers.

Ch. Tailspin Jupiter of Harobed, owned by Rose Levy of Harobed Cattery in Plainview, New York. Photo by Miceli Studios Ltd.

Two-month-old Flame and Tortie Point kittens bred and owned by Ruth Kitsmiller of Simi Valley, California.

Kit's Red Roar, seven-month-old Flame Point Himalayan bred and owned by Ruth Kitsmiller of Simi Valley, California.

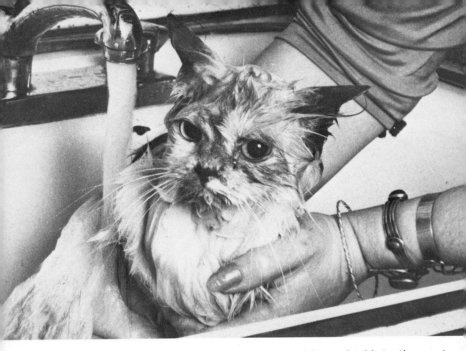

After shampoo and lather have been thoroughly worked into the coat, an equally thorough rinsing is essential. Water from the tap or a rubber spray hose can be used. It is *essential* that all soap be removed from the coat.

When the cat is dry and all tangles have been removed, go over the entire cat with a comb. Make sure the cat is one hundred per cent dry or it will pick up dirt — and maybe a cold — and another bath may be necessary!

During the entire bathing procedure talk to your cat and try to reassure it. Take time during the process to scratch its ears and rub under the chin or in other places which please your cat under ordinary circumstances. It won't be easy, but try to make the bath a time of communication with the cat rather than a task that must be done whether the cat likes it or not. Many cat owners I know try a "dry run" for a couple of days ahead of time. They go through the entire procedure without actually using soap and water. It does help to have the cat used to the sound of the dryer! And perhaps the most important helpful hint of all: be sure to cut the cat's nails before you start!

After rinsing, wrap the cat in a heavy turkish towel to absorb excess dripping. Then take a second turkish towel and squeeze the cat dry gently.

Above left: Sarobi Casanova, first in Kitten Classes at Kensington show, first in Colourpoint Class in Brussels and First in Class at Antwerp shows in 1973. Bred and owned by Mrs. Sheila A. Hughes of Sarobi Cattery, Folkestone, Kent, England. *Above right:* Archimedes, an 11-month old neutered Seal Point male in a lovely sylvan setting at his home, the Tomany Cattery. The cattery is owned by his breeder-owner, Mary Van Liew of Kew Gardens, Long Island, New York.

Robrick Isan at seven months of age. This lovely Blue Point female was sired by R. M. Ch. Chestermere Taki of Robrick *ex* R. M. Double Ch. Pitts Treasure of Robrick. Owned by P. A. Buell of Mission, B.C., Canada.

The Himalayan is much in demand because of its beautiful coat and attractive markings and also because of its excellent disposition. The lovely Himalayan here shown with the author is owned by Rose Levy of Harobed Cattery in Plainview, New York. Photo by Miceli Studios Ltd.

DRY BATHS

Talcum powder or cornstarch spread through the coat and then brushed right out again can sometimes eliminate the necessity for a regular bath, especially with kittens who get dirty walking through their food or the mud or the litter pan. When showing kittens, French chalk brushed into the coat will make the coat look even fluffier and beautiful. Just be sure that all traces of powder or chalk are brushed out of the coat before entering the show ring, or you may be disqualified.

These dry baths are helpful when a cat has dirtied itself in the litter pan or has gotten food into its coat while eating. Such soil must be removed or it will stain the coat.

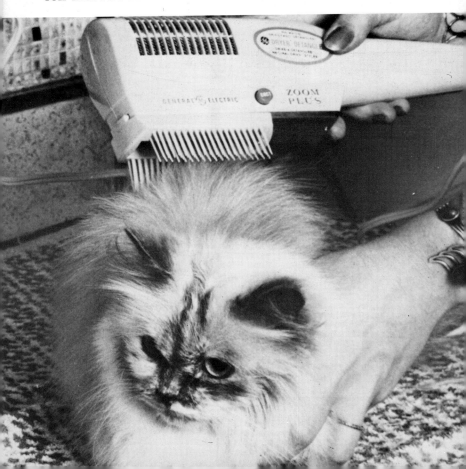

Once the cat is completely dry, a coat conditioner will give the final touch of beauty! Simply apply and brush into coat lightly for the perfect sheen.

Opposite:
Leave the cat on the towel and "blow dry" with an electric dryer attachment set on "warm air." Fluff the hair as you go, keeping the hair resting in the direction it should be naturally.

International Champion Mingchiu Mandarin of Sahadi, Seal Point male imported by the author after he had completed his championship in England, Scotland and Wales. Within a short time after being imported, this excellent stud cat achieved his championship in the United States as well, making him the first — and to date the only — champion on both sides of the Atlantic. (Many European cats are called "International Champion" on the basis of their having achieved championship status in more than one European nation, but they don't have pan-oceanic championship status.) Mandarin was sired by Briarry Valparago *ex* Briarry Roxanna. Born March 13, 1964; died April 13, 1974.

Oppos
Ready for the show ri
The finished product of pro
bathing leaves the cat beautifully clean
groomed and owner Jane Levy none
worse for w

Royal Merit Ch. Robrick Woodsprite, two-year-old blue Point female owned by Mr. and Mrs. Paul A. Buell of Mission, B.C., Canada. Woodsprite was Third Best Cat Northwestern Region according to the Himalayan Society and the ACFA Parade of Royalty. Sire was R. M. Ch. Chestermere Taki of Robrick ex R. M. Double Ch. Pitt's Treasure of Robrick.

Chapter 9
BUYING A KITTEN

All kittens are cute, and your choice should be based on some concrete objectives which you hope to achieve in the breed. After deciding that the Himalayan is the breed that you desire most and that it will fit into your family-style of living, there are certain preliminaries which should be taken care of.

Presumably you have read about the breed in cat magazines or books purchased at the pet shops, and hopefully you have actually seen some of them at the cat shows in your area. Also, you should have written to the cat organization of your choice to request their literature, and with an idea of joining a local cat club in the near future.

Then it is time to visit some of the local catteries with a copy of the Standard for the breed with you to see how close the parents of the kittens come to meeting it! Check out pedigrees, request photographs and show records, and try to ascertain from other breeders if they treat their cats kindly and maintain a clean cattery. A telephone or written inquiry to the owner should insure an appointment if the breeder is reputable and has nothing to hide.

Plan to visit the kittens when they are from 6 to 8 weeks old. They should not be allowed to leave the mother any time before this age. Look for clear eyes, shiny coat, unclogged nose, clean ears, clear skin, no parasites and no odor. The kits should play easily and feel well fed. Well fed means that the bones are well covered all over the body, not just a fat stomach!

Make certain the kittens are not deaf and that they move freely without limping or walking in a constant crouch and that they do not act scary all the time.

Beware of kittens that at this tender age run around "spitting" at people or at other cats or constantly raise their hackles or fluff up their tails at every little thing. Kittens that are "testy" at this early age usually do not make even-tempered companions after they grow up.

Ch. X.O.X. Betula, owned by the Copplestone Cattery of Mrs. I. Bentinck of Berkshire, England. Photography by Sally Anne Thompson.

Ask about the diet the kittens have been raised on, whether they have had any inoculations or serum protection, whether they have been wormed or have suffered from any infectious diseases. In observing the litter, determine which are the males and the females and make your decision as to which sex and which color you prefer. This will aid the breeder in narrowing down your choice.

SEXING KITTENS

The best and most knowledgeable breeders make mistakes

when trying to determine which are the males and which are the females. It is very difficult to determine sex in young kittens. However, if you are dealing with people who know cats, it is wisest to take their word for it, or a veterinarian's if sex is important to your plans.

The most successful way to determine the sex is to remember that when viewing the vent, or rear area of the kitten, the male will appear to have two small vertically placed spots beneath the tail, which resemble a colon (:). The female features an upside down exclamation point (!). Good luck, and if in doubt, get *several* other opinions!

Ch. Hima Tab Tango, Blue Point female owned by Mrs. LaVerne Grusell of Ashland, Ohio.

VETERINARY APPROVAL

When you have made your selection, post-date a check to cover your 24-hour veterinary approval. The reliable breeder will allow you to take the kitten to a veterinary of your choice to determine the good health of the kitten. If all is okay you are ready to welcome the newest member to your family. In the days that follow you can transfer papers and ownership so that the kitten will be truly and completely yours!

An adorable kitten from the Hima Tab Cattery, owned by Mrs. LaVerne Grusell of Ashland, Ohio.

Peyton Place Kay-Si, Seal Point Himalayan owned by Ann Peyton of Ventura, California. Photo by Earle Russell.

THE NEW KITTEN AT HOME

The new kitten should immediately be introduced to the area where it will be fed — and feed it next to the litter pan until you are sure it can find both places! Be sure fresh water is there also and a bed if you choose to give it one other than your own. Do not forget the toys and a scratching post. And do not forget to keep an eye on the kitten to see that it is protected from danger and that it is properly introduced to any other animals in the family circle.

BUYING ADULT STOCK

If it is necessary to buy adult stock to advance your cattery breeding program, or even to increase your personal menagerie, it would be wise to take along another breeder. Here again, make sure papers are in order, that the records of breedings and wins at the shows are accurate and up-to-date, and that the cat has a clean bill of health. If you want to breed make sure the stud and queen are proven and their record of healthy kittens is impressive. If acquired on breeding terms, make sure a signed contract agreeable to both seller and buyer and stating all requirements is in order.

Additional time should be given to introducing the grown cat into the household, allowing plenty of time for adjustment to the new surroundings before expecting the cat to start breeding.

Triple Champion Crestvue's Little Star of Shahi Taj, Blue Point female co-owned by W. O. Walsh and W. J. Andruscavage of the Shahi Taj Cattery in Dayton, Virginia. Photo by M. K. Walsh.

Chapter 10
BREEDING
YOUR HIMALAYAN

Unfortunately every year in the United States hundreds of thousands of unwanted kittens and puppies (and dogs and cats!) are put to sleep as a result of the greatest animal over-population the world has ever known; we must all think twice before we consider having a litter.

Unless you have a specific, planned breeding program in mind, using pure-bred animals for which you already have interested new owners, I must suggest you forget breeding cats entirely . . . or at least enter into it with great caution. Bringing additional kittens into the world without providing proper homes for them is unconscionable.

We have long since passed the day when we could use the excuse that parents really believe that having a litter is a good way for their children to learn about birth and motherhood. The sole purpose of breeding a litter of kittens should be the desire to better the breed or to perpetuate a valuable bloodline to carry on the breed in the future.

If you can be sure this is your intent in the fancy and that the result of your planned breeding will bring quality kittens with a healthy, happy future in store for them, you might do well to go ahead with your plan — but still *not* before giving additional thought to some other considerations.

THE MASTER PLAN

If your breeding program is sound and the pedigrees promise a compatible combination of bloodlines known to produce quality kittens, there are still other very important and practical considerations to be taken into account before the actual mating takes place.

First and very important is the consideration of money. Are you prepared for the expenses involved in paying a stud fee and veterinary bills for inoculations or any complications which might occur during gestation and after birth? There will be the extra expense for proper additional foods and vitamins for both the mother and the growing kittens, as well as their maintenance until the kittens are sold.

Then ask yourself whether you are prepared to be in attendance at the time of delivery to see that all goes well for the queen and the kittens. You cannot disregard the birth date because you have heard cats are easy whelpers and good mothers. If you are away from home for long periods of time, or both members of the family work and the children are out to school all day, DO NOT BREED. Unless, that is, you are prepared to have a full-time cat-sitter in attendance . . . which can be expensive.

Also, you might pose the question as to whether or not you are prepared to devote the time to socializing the kittens and to finding them the devoted owners and proper homes we mentioned earlier. Is your cattery or home large enough to offer the space and facilities for properly raising active kittens that spend so much time exercising and at play? Are you prepared to go to any expense — or any distance — required to obtain the best possible stud service insuring a worthwhile litter? Are you willing to assume the additional expense of registering the litter and the kittens to assure their eligibility in the show ring?

If you are prepared to meet these and any other unforeseen problems which might arise, it is time to plan ahead on your breeding, and with a clear conscience.

SELECTING THE STUD

There are many ways to find the correct stud for your cat. The breeder of your cat might have a suggestion as to what lines would "nick" well with her bloodlines from past experience. You can attend cat shows and discuss bloodlines of the winning cats in your breed. You might inquire as to what results have been achieved by other breeders who also have your bloodlines or have purchased stock from the same breeder you did. Or you might consult with a well-known and respected judge who is reputed to be especially knowledgeable in the breed.

Grand Champion Nevah-Tep's Vogue, bred and owned by Boris Teron and Larry Keely of Chicago.

THE STUD FEE

The usual financial requirement for a breeding is called a stud fee and is decided by the owner of the stud. The more wins and the more successful breedings of good quality kittens, the greater the fee. Most breeders prefer a fee — especially if their cat is used a great deal — since they cannot be expected to take a "pick of litter" kitten on every breeding. However, if your queen is equally desirable and possesses important bloodlines, the owner of the stud may be perfectly willing to breed on a "kitten" basis. It is usually for what they consider "pick of the litter" at around 6 to 8 weeks, or it can be for pick of the males or pick of the females, depending on whether they expect to sell the kitten or reintroduce it, and your bloodline, back into their breeding program.

If they have a waiting list for kittens, they may consent to let you keep the top male and female in the litter to start your cattery off with top quality stock, and then be willing to take either the rest of the kittens in the litter or a specified number they believe to be fair. It must be remembered that such a contract is determined according to the wants of each party involved. There is no set standard contract. However, even though breedings can be negotiated between the interested parties it is certainly recommended that any qualifications be made in writing with both parties signing the contract.

THE CONTRACT

The contract need not be highly official or complicated. It can be a simply stated document outlining what each point is to satisfy the owner of the stud and then the signature of agreement to the terms by the owner of the queen.

It is also important in any contract to specify whether or not a return service is to be granted should the initial mating not produce any kittens. It is also wise to add the word "live" kittens. A stillborn litter constitutes a litter of kittens in some people's minds but will do the owner of the queen no good at all as far as her breeding program goes. How long the litter must remain "living" is also a point of order. Usually a matter of days is all that should be required, since any loss of the litter could possibly be the fault of the queen as well as the stud.

However, we repeat — get it all in writing, since many a friendship has been lost during the emotional period of whelping and raising a litter. When terms are written down any third party can easily interpret the requirements it contained.

PAYMENT OF THE FEE

You will be expected to pay the fee at the time of the breeding, usually when you go to pick up your queen, unless, of

Royal Merit and Quadruple Champion Emindale's Sunshine of Shahi Taj, Flame Point female, owned by W. O. Walsh of Dayton, Virginia. Sunshine's 1974 show awards are as follows: Best Cat, Southern Region (Him. Soc.); Best Himalayan in Virginia; Best Flame Point, Southern Region; Best Flame Point in Virginia; Best Flame Point, Southern Region (CFA); Best Opposite Sex, Southern Region (CFF); Best Flame Point, Southern Region; Royal Regional HM Female of Breed (ACFA); Royal Regional Female of Color of Breed; *Cats Magazine* Award.

course, there has been some other acceptable condition of payment which should also be clearly stated in the contract.

CHOOSE WISELY

If your queen is a highly valuable cat, or even if you are just a devoted owner trying to move up in the degree of perfection in your line, you would do well to be sure you are dealing with reputable owners. Feel free to inquire into their show win record, determine in advance that the cattery is a clean,

Double Grand and Sextuple Ch. Mingchiu Pearlas of Harobed and her first litter of Himalayan kittens. Imported and owned by Rose Levy, Plainview, Long Island, New York.

disease-free cattery with adequate facilities for visiting queens, and do not hesitate to ask about the diet they offer.

You must remember that you will have to bring that queen back into your own place when the breeding is over, and you do not want her bringing back fleas, worms, infectious diseases, etc. A reliable breeder or owner will be happy to "brag" about their method of rearing and caring for their cats and will welcome a reputation of providing well for visiting queens to help them build up a reputation for their stud cat. Beware of owners who want to take your queen at the door and tell you to return in a few days.

You must also believe them to be truthful in their practices and that your queen will be bred to the stud of your choice and not put with another male on the premises to take some of the "pressure" off their popular stud that might be considered too good for your less than top quality queen. This has been known to happen but is almost impossible to prove, so be sure the stud's owner is beyond reproach.

Mingchiu Dorian, photographed as a kitten in July of 1964 before being imported to the United States by Rose Levy, Harobed Cattery, Plainview, Long Island, New York. Breeder, Mrs. S. M. Harding, England.

THE BREEDING SEASON

From three to six times each year your female, or queen, will come into season. This "heat" will be recognized by some very positive, very obvious, actions on her part, when she reaches anywhere from five to seven months of age. You will suddenly become aware of the fact that she is washing herself more frequently than usual, will be more affectionate than ever, will urinate more frequently, and will roll on the floor erratically, back and forth from side to side repeatedly. She will also crouch down on her front feet while treading with her back feet with her hind end and tail in an "up periscope" position.

This behavior will be accompanied by her vocal expression or "calling." The sound range of the "calling" will be anywhere from a low rumble to a constantly repeated high-pitched howl. This calling will last anywhere from three days to two weeks, and there will be no mistaking it from the usual vocal conversations one has with female cats.

While the male is always ready to breed — and answers the call — you will know that the onset of this erratic behavior indicates that she is ready to be put with the male of your choice for a period of cohabitation.

THE MATING

Usually the cats prefer to breed at night when it is dark and there is no audience or interference. Many of the more experienced stud cats no longer have a desire for such privacy and will simply grab the queen by the back of the neck and cover her no matter what, who, when or where. But it is advisable to give them every consideration for a successful breeding, especially when dealing with an inexperienced queen. Achieving a successful breeding is, after all, the main objective, not the aplomb or speed with which the stud conducts himself.

The actual mating is a rather quick process, but the breeding act should be repeated several times to insure success. Therefore, it is wise to cage them together for a period of days to

Hima-Shell Blue Angel with points toward championship has temporarily retired from the show ring to have a litter. Owned by Michelle Woods, Hima-Shell Cattery, Palos Hills, Illinois.

achieve success. It is unlikely that you will not know when and if they breed, since the queen will usually snarl and spit (sometimes even attack the male) once he releases his hold on the back of her neck. The breeding is painful for the queen, since the male has "barbs" on his penis which scratch her as he removes himself from her. This cry after a successful mating is usually followed by her frantically rolling and tossing herself from side to side once again, followed by their both retiring to "neutral corners" to clean themselves.

The female's attack on the male often frightens those who have not observed this behavior before or those who see it for the first time. But it is seldom damaging or of long duration and must be accepted as part of the ritual and put in proper perspective. Owners of stud cats who see it for the first time are often bewildered by the sudden change in behavior of their dominant stud turning into a cowering "pussycat" when the female turns on him. And lucky are those owners whose studs

Hima Tab Peg O'My Heart, Blue Point female photographed at five weeks of age. Bred and owned by Mrs. LaVerne Grusell of Hima Tab Cattery, Ashland, Ohio.

are always "pussycats" and ignore the assault with a bat of an eye and yet accomplish their mission time after time .

There is a lot to be said for tolerance and experience — even in the cat world.

CARE OF THE QUEEN

Once the breeding has been accomplished it is time to relax until the tenth day. At this point it is wise to add extra vitamins and milk to the diet, on a gradually increasing scale. Your veterinarian is the best one to advise you of the types and amounts for your individual cat, as well as give you the proper strength worm medicine for worming before the third week of pregnancy. Worm medicine today is a well researched preparation, but many veterinarians recommend not worming at all if the cat does not show evidence of worms. Here again, when inquiring about your diet supplements, test for parasites, and get your worm medicine — if necessary — at the same time.

GESTATION

Kittens require 63 to 65 days gestation and usually the first litter is early. Be prepared for early arrivals! I do not mean to imply it is necessary to hover over the queen like a nervous mother hen, but be prepared for birth a week ahead of the 65 days normally required.

By being prepared I mean have the veterinarian's telephone number next to the telephone in case you need him, have a tray with scissors for cutting cords if she doesn't, and paper towels for drying kittens if you have to be of help to her during repeated arrivals. Kittens sometimes arrive so quickly the queen does not have time to finish with one kitten before another comes.

Cats usually are easy, quiet whelpers and it will probably all be over before you hear the first meow. But it never hurts to be ready just in case. The queen usually will have chosen the place where she wants to have her kittens, and you will be wise not to try to change it. It will only distress her. If she is not caged, it will more than likely be the darkest, most quiet and most inaccessible spot she can find. It is in this secluded atmosphere that she will choose to have her litter. Litters usually average three to five kittens.

If she is a caged cat she should be given a cardboard box with plenty of newspapers to scratch up to make a nest. She should be allowed the privacy and quiet she would normally seek if she were allowed to roam free. Even cats that are never caged could possibly do better in a cage at this time. If there is any difficulty the owner has easy access to the box to aid her and will always know where she is in case trouble comes after the delivery.

The first few days after birth she will remain with her kits, or very close by, and around the third day you will notice that she has already established a schedule for reentering the box when the kits should be fed. It is around this time that she will not resent intervention or the handling of the kittens and will almost welcome personal admiration and praise. The purring and the opening and contracting of the claws at this time will be highly noticeable and the signal that all is well with the queen and her new babies.

Mingchiu Carlo, another of the beautiful kittens bred at Mrs. S. M. Harding's cattery in England.

NEWBORN KITTENS

Himalayan kittens — the same as Siamese kittens — are born white all over with pink nose and pad leather. Within the first week the pigmentation starts filling in; within a matter of a few weeks you can be almost certain what color the points will be. You will know how well you succeeded with your "planned" color breeding.

Your Seal Point and Blue Point kittens will get color sooner than the Chocolate or Lilac Points, and you should be able to

Grand Champion Di-Or Angelique of Hima-Tab, winner of the 1968 CFA Hydon-Goodwin award, as Best Blue Point Himalayan. Angelique was the second female Himalayan to make a CFA Grand Championship.

determine which is which within a month. Certainly before they are ready to go to their new owners at eight weeks.

Many breeders delight in weighing and measuring kittens, but it is of greater importance that all kittens in the litter grow uniformly and at a steady even pace, rather than what their actual body weight adds up to on the scale. Kittens at birth average two to four ounces and usually double this weight the first week to ten days. Here again variances occur according to the number of kittens in the litter and how well each kitten eats.

Any loss of weight with one particluar kitten may indicate the need for supplemental feeding. However, because of the large number of inexperienced breeders and owners who attempt tube feeding and insert the tube into the lungs instead of the stomach, or over-feed, we will not attempt to instruct in tube feeding techniques in this book. Your veterinarian may wish to instruct you in this if he deems it necessary, but in any case the decision should be his.

Eyes will open between the fifth and the tenth day, and extreme bright light should be avoided near the whelping box. If there seems to be a delay or gummy, stuck-shut eyes on a particular kitten in the litter, the advice of a veterinarian seems to be in order.

SOCIALIZING THE NEWBORN KITTENS

The first few weeks of a kitten's life are the most informative. During this period the kitten should be handled extensively by experienced hands, should experience as many types of flooring and carpeting as possible and be cuddled and talked to by all. A kitten that is frequently and *kindly* handled and appreciated will grow up to be a much better adjusted animal than the kitten that is allowed to fend for itself and not experience human companionship. This socialization is essential if your cat is to be a show cat, and will make even the pet cat a better adjusted member of a family or an outdoor feline society if it is an outdoor cat.

WEANING AND FEEDING THE KITTENS

Weaning is usually at about three to six weeks, assuming there has been supplemental feeding or that the kittens were allowed to eat from their mother's dish. While they are still nursing and getting their required mother's milk, wean them on the strained baby foods, such as beef, lamb and veal. This can be licked from your finger in the beginning. As they stay less and less with the mother cat, introduce them to milk consisting of ⅔ evaporated milk with ⅓ water, with honey, raw egg yolk and wheat germ added. Goat milk is the very best to feed when they move on to whole milk, but it is expensive and not always available except through drug stores.

Unless you have a good supply of it, stay with the evaporated a little longer than you would ordinarily, and then switch to the whole milk or light cream with their baby cereal or pablum. Milk sometimes has a laxative effect if not served at *room* temperature! In fact, all foods and liquids should be served at room temperature. Anything too cold or too hot will tend to physic a cat or a kitten. So it is wise to get in the habit of serving food and drinking water at a moderate temperature, and insure against chilling the stomach and causing cramps or undue distress. Kitten chow and other foods are added gradually as the kittens grow used to solid foods.

It is wise to keep the kittens with the mother cat for as long as she will tolerate them, since there is really no perfect substitute for mother's milk.

VACCINATIONS

Before the kittens are ready to go to their new homes at about eight weeks of age they should have had a protective "shot." Depending on the size and weight and age of the kittens, the veterinarian can best prescribe the type and amount of serum to protect them until the time comes for more permanent protection. However, be sure to tell the new owner about the type and amount of serum your veterinarian administered when you provide the pedigree and registration papers.

REGISTERING THE KITTENS

After the litter is born a litter registration form should be obtained from the organization with which you want to register them. This form should then be filled in completely with all required particulars and sent with the fee to the registry of your choice. They in turn will process the information and send you a litter registration kit with a number for your litter and individual registration blanks for each kitten.

Some breeders prefer to register each kitten individually so that they may select full names for each. Other breeders will only insist on their registered cattery prefix being included and will allow the new owner to write in the name of his choice immediately following the cattery name. Whichever the procedure, these forms should then be returned with the fee to the cat registry to transfer the ownership of the cat or kitten and permanently record the name of the animal along with all the other vital statistics.

It is essential that the breeder impress upon the new owner the importance of keeping these papers in order. They will be necessary if the kitten is to be shown or if it is to be resold at some future date, and essential also if the cat is to be bred.

FADING KITTEN SYNDROME

One of the heartbreaks of having a litter is suddenly to see the kittens die — one after another. This disease, or syndrome, which plagues a great many breeders in spite of all the miraculous strides in veterinary research is referred to as the fading kitten syndrome. Veterinarians admit they do not know for certain what is the cause nor do they know a cure. It is thought to be a virus infection of some kind, but a positive answer has not yet been found.

It usually occurs during the first few weeks of life when tragedy strikes what has up to this time been apparently a normal healthy kitten. The kitten simply stops eating, hunches up in a corner and silently dies. Sometimes the entire litter is wiped out, sometimes only one or more are affected. But once it hits, no drug or supplemental feeding or tender loving care can bring it back.

Unfortunately, kittens can also die from various other causes. Some might be through the queen or from other cats in the cattery or in the home. Healthy kittens actually appear to be thriving with a steady rate of growth, and it doesn't take long for an interested breeder to notice trouble in the litter. Needless to say, immediate veterinary advice is indicated if any of the litter is to be saved, and even it the mother is lost it is possible to raise a litter of kittens on bottle feedings.

THE DAY OF SALE

You and you alone must bear the responsibility of finding the ideal home for your kittens. The queen has completed her end of the bargain by giving you a fine litter; now it is up to the breeder to place them properly. Proper placement will not only be for the good of the kittens but will carry on your cattery name by presenting it to the public in the show ring or by being an ideal, well adjusted family pet.

You are further obligated to provide the new owner with a healthy kitten with its papers in order, basic grooming and feeding information and the opportunity to take it to the new owner's veterinarian for a health check within 24 hours. Any congenital or health defects will require that you take the kitten back.

PRICE OF THE KITTEN

Prices vary depending on age, bloodlines, and whether or not it is to be a show cat or just a pet, so any figure written here would be sheer guesswork. It varies individually from cattery to cattery, but it goes without saying that show cats or show-quality kittens are more expensive than just an ordinary pure-bred kitten. If you are not familiar with the current market prices, make a point of calling a few other catteries advertising in the newspapers or cat magazines and establish a top and low price on the kittens. In other words, what you believe them to be worth and the very least you will take for them without destroying the "going market price," or under-selling the breed.

CONDITIONS OF SALE

If you wish to attach any conditions to the sale of the kittens or even one kitten in the litter, this is the time to get it on the record. Get all terms and conditions of the sale in writing, signed by both parties — as with the stud fee — and protect yourself in the future. It is sometimes wise to sell the kitten for a cash price plus a stud service on a male cat, or a kitten on a future litter with a female. That way, if they turn out to be something sensational you will not have cut yourself off entirely from the bloodlines in your own litter.

If you sell with "strings attached," however, it is only fair that some adjustment be made in the price, since newcomers to a breed may become discouraged if they have to worry about future obligations on a cat that they have paid well to love and own in its own right.

Just remember above all that verbal contracts are seldom satisfactory — even among friends!

SPAYING AND CASTRATION

If kittens are not to be included in your future plans, the best time to spay a female is between five and six months. This will avoid a first season usually and keep male cats from your door, while keeping her content to stay at home.

The best time to neuter a male is eight months or any time thereafter. This will prevent his spraying or wandering off in search of female companionship.

The stories that neutering and spaying cats changes their disposition and makes them fat and lazy are simply old wives' tales! They have no basis in fact. If your neuter or spay gets fat it's because it is either overfed or does not exercise enough.

The judging setup for the 1972 Molates, Sweden cat show; in the foreground is Longhair judge Mrs. Edel Ringsted from Denmark with an apprentice judge, and three stewards. Arrow indicates Mrs. Irma Tingwell, one of the first to start the initial cat club in Sweden in 1946. She is still actively showing cats.

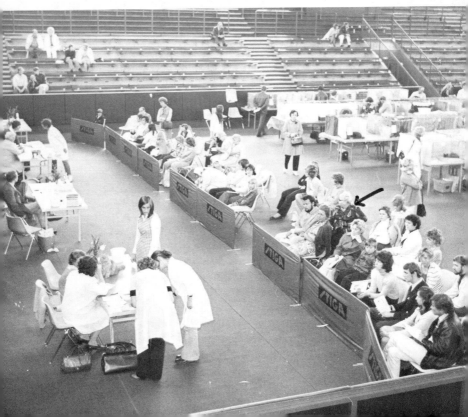

Chapter 11
CAT ASSOCIATIONS, CAT CLUBS, AND CAT PUBLICATIONS

CAT ASSOCIATIONS IN THE UNITED STATES

The cat fancy in America has a number of associations which register cats and act as governing bodies. The most important and the largest of these is the Cat Fanciers Association, Inc., situated at Red Bank, New Jersey. Their member clubs are listed in the hundreds; the president, Richard Gebhardt, is the most prominent person in the cat world. Under his jurisdiction and leadership great strides have been accomplished in the fancy in every phase of operation. Their annual *Yearbook* has become an important permanent hard-cover volume of the fancy for each 12-month period and their quarterly publication provides valuable information four times a year. The annual meeting, held each June in a different area of the nation, is attended by hundreds, and a program of activities excites the interest of all who love cats and show them.

Several of the other associations have been active for many years also but have much fewer clubs and are active in more restricted areas. These include the Cat Fanciers Federation, or CFF, the American Cat Fanciers Association (ACFA), another of the earlier ones, the National Cat Fanciers Association (NCFA,) the American Cat Association (ACA,) the United Cat Fanciers (UCF,) the Independent Cat Fanciers (ICF,) and the latest, Crown Cat Fanciers Federation, known briefly as Crown .

UNITED STATES CAT CLUBS

Cat clubs which comprise the member organizations in the

above-mentioned associations are far too numerous to mention here. However, all are to be commended on their ultimate goals in improving the lives and welfare of cats and in their presentation to the cat-loving public through their cat shows and breeding programs.

CAT CLUBS IN ENGLAND

Great Britain is one of the most active countries in the fancy, however, the six-month quarantine law in Great Britain prohibits outsiders from showing cats in that country. The Governing Council of the Cat Fancy, referred to simply as the GCCF, boasts its own rules and regulations and sets its own Standards for perfection. It was formed in 1910.

The cat shows themselves are also conducted and judged on a completely different basis from the rest of the world. In Britain the judges visit the benching areas and pass judgment on the cats. When the ribbons have been hung and their judgments recorded, the public is admitted to view the awards.

Cats and cat shows enjoy tremendous popularity in England and always have, from the days of the first Crystal Palace show in 1871, with an entry of 160 cats. The National Cat Club show, held in the National Hall in Olympia, is perhaps the largest of all and boasts entries of almost two thousand each December.

The National Cat Club was the first British cat club. The second club was formed by Lady Marcus Beresford in 1898 and today there are over 65 clubs, most of which are represented by the GCCF.

The GCCF is composed of delegates appointed annually by the members of the various affiliated clubs; the delegates receive no fees for their services. The Council employs two registrars to handle the registrations and transfers and a secretary to handle general business and correspondence. It issues the stud books and grants licenses for shows held under its jurisdiction, approves Standards for new varieties of cats and gives challenge and premier certificates at championship shows.

THE HIMALAYAN IN ENGLAND

The Colourpoint Longhair, as the Himalayan is called in England, was first recognized by the GCCF in 1955.

THE FEDERATION INTERNATIONAL FELINE

The Federation International Feline, or FIFE as it is known generally, was established in 1949. In the pre-World War II years there was an earlier forerunner group founded in France in 1932 with the help of Italian and Swiss fanciers. They established rules and regulations and certain Standards adopted from English lines. After the war they reorganized, and again with Italian and Swiss help an organization with new incentives was once again active. Soon Belgium was a member, and then the Scandinavian countries expressed interest in becoming members.

By the time the 1973 Assemblee Generale was held in Switzerland, 12 European countries had become members of FIFE: France, Italy, Switzerland, Belgium, Austria, Holland, Denmark, Germany, Sweden, Norway, Finland and Czechoslovakia. At the Assemblee Generale in 1972 the Brazilian club (Clube Brasileiro Do Gato) was voted into membership and became the first club from another continent to join. At the 1973 Assemblee, the Australian National Cat Federation became a member also, and yet another continent became represented. More nations are to be represented in the future as well, and have already expressed interest.

In the FIFE organization each country keeps its own stud books, but FIFE keeps its own supervisory book which contains the names of all catteries. This is the job of the Secretary. Each country has one delegate and runs its own cat shows. FIFE has three boards: the directing board, judging board, and the show and disciplinary board, each consisting of six to eight people. Each country may hold as many shows as it wishes, but the shows must be separated by a specified distance. There are Championship Certificate award requirements, and to become a full National Champion a cat has to be winner of its breed and sex in the open Class and gain the Champion Certificate three times under three different judges. To become a full International Champion a cat has to be awarded the International Champion Certificate three times under three different judges, and one of the certificates has to be won abroad.

Unlike as in the United States and England, the custom is that winning cats receive ribbons, cups, challenge certificates or other tokens, but not money. Judges do not receive money either. The judging assignment is to be considered an honor, though all judging expenses are paid.

CAT CLUBS IN JAPAN

Interest in purebred cats in Japan is keen and increases with each passing year. The Japan Cat Fanciers Association invites American judges to officiate at their major show each year, and there are members of the Cat Fanciers Association here in the United States who work very closely with the Japanese in every phase of their operation. The Japanese red carpet treatment is given their judges, who are very active in club affairs in their own country. They import a great many cats and also export some of their own breeding, especially Japanese Bobtails. American judges attest to the quality of Japanese cats and breeding programs.

Since Japanese weather is comparable to our New England states, longhaired cats are popular and do well in Japan.

The 79-year-old Mrs. Shirane is president of the Japan Cat Fanciers Association and she and her husband are largely responsible for the popularity cats are being given in that country.

In 1972 the Cat Fanciers of Hokkaido club was formed; there are, as of 1975, four C.F.A. all-breed cat clubs in Japan.

CAT CLUBS IN SCANDINAVIA

Scandinavian countries judge shows similar to U.S. rules and are members of FIFE. Their judging is conducted with the public present and with several judging areas being conducted at the same time.

CAT CLUBS IN GERMANY

The governing cat association in Germany is the Deutscher Edelkatzenzuchterverband. The association is a member of FIFE, of course, and is active on the International Committee of the Cat Fanciers Association, Inc. in America.

CAT CLUBS IN AUSTRALIA

In Australia the governing body is called the Feline Association of Southern Australia. They also are members of the International Committee of the Cat Fanciers Association, Inc. in America.

CAT CLUBS IN CANADA

There is the Canadian Cat Association, referred to as CCA, for our Canadian neighbors; the CCA requires that all cats to be shown in their country be registered individually with them. They do not recognize American registrations.

Many cats from the United States are shown at their shows and capture top wins, and many top Canadian cats are shown in the United States.

JOINING A CAT CLUB

It is wise to join at least one cat club, especially if you intend to show or if you have just gotten your first cat. Clubs offer a wealth of information on cats in all phases of development. Most clubs have newsletters or publications and pamphlets of some kind which will help you care for your cat and keep you posted on what is new in the fancy. Whichever organization you choose to register with, the corresponding secretary can supply you with the name and address of the charter club in your area.

CAT PUBLICATIONS

There are several periodical sources from which to obtain

news and information about cats; you will find any or all of these publications of great value to you in helping to keep a healthy happy cat, and I suggest you subscribe to one or more of the publications in the magazine field. If you write to them, chances are they will be happy to send you a sample copy along with subscription information:

CATS Magazine — Raymond Smith, editor
   P.O. Box 4106
   Pittsburgh, Pennsylvania 15202

CAT FANCY — Bruce Sessions, Editor
   248 S. Robertson Boulevard
   Beverly Hills, California 90211

The judging area at a cat show in Japan. A judge holds up a cat to observe certain characteristics as the woman behind her explains the requirements for the Standard for the breed. Several assistants, sitting at the end of the table, await an opportunity to assist the judge by cleaning cages, readying ribbons to be awarded, etc.

CAT WORLD — Sid and Pauline Thompson, editors
5395 South Miller Street
Littleton, Colorado 80123

ALL CATS — Will Thompson, editor
15113 Sunset Boulevard
Pacific Palisades, California 90272

CFA YEARBOOK — Joan Brearley, editor
Box 430
Red Bank, N.J. 07701

The *Cat Fanciers Association Yearbook* is a hard-cover, yearly publication covering a complete record of the activities in the cat world.

In addition to the above magazines and yearbook, there are several newsletters and club bulletins of special interest to Himalayan owners:

Himalayan World — Garth Watkins, editor
P.O. Box 6247
San Mateo, California 94403

International Himalayan Society Bulletin
Dodie G. Wilcox, editor
1436 W. Montrose,
Chicago, Illinois 60613

The Himalayan Society Bulletin
Elaine Wagner, editor
1549 North Highland
Arlington Heights, Illinois 60004

International European
Champion and International
Premier Briarry Nigella,
Blue Point Himalayan,
pictured with her owner, Mrs.
Brita Kastengren-Remborg
of Sweden. Mrs. Remborg is
a famous international judge
of cats in both Europe
and the United States.

Chapter 12
SHOWING
YOUR HIMALAYAN

One day you take a good hard look at your Himalayan and are impressed with the quality of the cat you see. You make a decision: your cat is an excellent specimen; it well represents the breed, and you want to make it a champion!

We assume that by now you have registered your cat or your litter, and it is time for you to write for literature regarding necessary information on upcoming shows and how to enter them. A calender of cat shows can be obtained from any of the cat magazines which publish not only coming shows but also the show win results of those which have been held. Or you may write for information from any of the individual cat organizations.

Since the various registering organizaions do not recognize each other's registrations, it is wise to select the one organization in which you wish to show and enter only their shows. Multiple registrations are allowed and many breeders, obsessed with the desire to attend cat shows every weekend and not caring how far they have to travel to do so, enter several of the associations. This method, however, involves endless paper work and many dollars spent in fees for the paper work involved and is especially not recommended for newcomers to the fancy. Wait and choose wisely and concentrate on success with one association. You can always branch out later if you want to, and in the meantime you will not have spent money for fees on registrations you will not want to use throughout your breeding program.

Disgruntled members who "break off" from their original club are largely responsible for the many associations we have today, and most do not amount to anything more than "just another association."

ENTERING A SHOW

You can enter your kitten in the *Kitten class* between the ages of four to eight months. If you do not enter a show until your cat is over eight months of age, it must be shown in the *Novice Class*, the class for cats which have never won a blue ribbon. Requirements for this class may vary with each organization, so be sure to read the show rules which will be used for the particular show you have entered.

Open Class is for cats over two years of age that have already won ribbons. Cats over two years of age MUST be entered in this class.

POINTS TOWARD CHAMPIONSHIP

Points won toward a championship are awarded according to the number of cats competing; points are determined on the day of the show.

CLASS PROCEDURE

Cats compete on a pyramid basis with other breeds. After competing within their own breed first, they ultimately compete for added wins and titles against the other breeds, with the top win being Best Cat in Show. Here again, each organization has its own special awards, though basically the same classes and pyramid system leads to the special top awards with their traditional array of ribbons, rosettes and trophies.

SHOW PSYCHOLOGY

Showing is sometimes said to be a hardship on a cat. However, if your cat is properly indoctrinated to show procedures, is used to being handled, used to riding in a car, used to periodic confinement in a cage and accustomed to other cats or other animals, a cat show will not faze it at all. And the trophies and awards you win along the way often help earn your cattery a good reputation for breeding quality stock as well as being a source of pride for you personally.

132

Grand Champion Kemlen Kala Haji, top-winning Blue Point Himalayan show cat owned by Georgia Kemp, Kemlen Cattery, Detroit, Michigan.

Mingchiu Dorian (on the left) and Mingchiu Mandella photographed at their home in England on July 29th, 1964. Dorian and Mandella were imported by Rose Levy and Joan Brearley, and shown in this country shortly after this photograph was taken. These beautiful Seal Point kittens were bred by Mrs. S. M. Harding.

At the same time you are exhibiting a quality cat you will also be helping to show the public what a good representative of the breed should look like. A beautiful cat in beautiful condition that wins well at a show will do a lot of good to the breed as well as helping to endear cats to everyone . . . and at the same time the cats will be getting the recognition they deserve from the judges!

THE DAY OF THE SHOW

Veterinary Inspection

When you arrive at the show you will be expected to go through the veterinary line. There will be one or more tables with a veterinarian at each to go over each cat as it enters the show hall and check it for disease or such things as fleas, ear mites, etc. Naturally it is unethical for anyone to bring an ailing cat to the show hall, but some crave the prizes or want the wins so badly they will try to sneak through the veterinary inspection to compete. The veterinarian has the right to forbid your cat or cats from entering the show hall. If there is a question about your cat's physical condition it is wise not to risk the embarrassment of being ejected from the show hall.

Many veterinarians refuse to "vet in" at a show, since they claim they cannot really give the cats a proper examination in so little time. The various organizations require that the show-giving clubs require their presence anyway, if only to ban the obvious symptoms of contagious disease and the equally obvious fleas, ear mites, etc.

Grooming At The Show

Most of the grooming should be done at home before the show. Only last-minute "touch-ups" should be necessary in the show hall, though it is wise to bring enough equipment to handle any emergency.

Essentials For Attending Shows

In addition to your grooming equipment you will need a well-ventilated carrier with appropriate lining. Paper or blanketing is good. You will need to bring water and food dishes and a litter box or pan if those things are not provided by the show committee. You will need cage curtains to line the cage at the show hall and a rug for the bottom of the cage if you do not wish to use the one from your carrier. A toy from home is a nice touch to help the cat enjoy itself, or one can be purchased from one of the concessions at the show. A lock for the cage is important, especially if your cat is to be left in the show hall overnight for the two-day shows. Others use pipe cleaners or wire twists used for plants, bread wrappers, etc.

Don't forget the food for the food dish, and bring your own thermos of water from home if your cat is inclined to become upset by "foreign" water. Don't be alarmed if your cat chooses to sleep during most of the show hours. Cats have a marvelous facility for shutting out the noise that goes on in a show hall as visitors wander up and down the aisles and exhibitors chatter about their wins or losses!

HARD-TO-HANDLE CATS

Even if you have an exceptionally good show cat, if there is any reason at all for you to believe that the cat will bite a judge, or *you*, or anyone else that might approach the cage, it is your OBLIGATION *NOT* TO SHOW THAT CAT!

Some stud cats are always hard to handle and become particularly difficult at shows when they detect the odor of other studs or queens in season. While most studs are still tractable enough to be handled and held by owner and judge, many others "blow" and bite viciously. It is not fair — or ethical — to subject a judge or anyone else to this danger. Cat bites are among the most painful and the most infectious of all animal bites and a cat bite is never to be taken lightly. An immediate washing out with soap and water is necessary, and it is wise to see a doctor right away.

Cats that become restless at shows, that are being campaigned week after week, or suffer from car sickness, etc., should be given periodic rests from competition. Persistent showing can jeopardize the good temperament of a cat and permanently affect its disposition.

AFTER THE SHOW

Some breeders, especially those with kittens at home, will keep an "isolation area" in their catteries where they keep cats after returning from a cat show, especially if they have reason to believe they have been exposed to disease or parasites at the show.

Any symptoms of infection will usually show up within 21 days, but if you believe there has been exposure, it would be wise to visit your veterinarian, even if no signs of disease are evident. Discuss with him your suspicions, and perhaps he will

Grand Champion Chestermere Chahila, bred by Ann and Ben Borrett of Canada, and owned and shown by Will Thompson of Burbank, California. Chahila was the top-winning Himalayan cat of all time: She was Best Cat in Show 41 times!

Royal Merit and Quadruple Champion Shahi Taj Hermione, a beautiful Seal Point female owned by W. O. Walsh of the Shahi Taj Cattery, Dayton, Virginia. Photo by M. K. Walsh.

suggest a booster shot to lighten the degree of infection your cat might have contracted.

Fungus, which can be picked up from unsterilized cages in the show hall, is the dread of all cat owners. Highly contagious even to humans, fungus can ruin a cat's coat and takes months to cure. It is the habit of most breeders to carry their own cage disinfectant to each show and wipe down the cage before putting the cat in it.

Chapter 13
COMMON AILMENTS

With good food and good care it is easily possible to have a healthy cat. But cats are also known, when exposed to infection, to be susceptible to various kinds of viral infections. Early inoculations usually preclude any serious diseases, but there are various infections which can prove bothersome and, if neglected, may become serious.

VIRAL INFECTIONS

Any clogging of the nose, runny eyes, diarrhea, temperature or loss of appetite indicates an infection and depending on the severity of symptoms, might require a trip to the veterinarian. Further inoculation of antibiotics or treatment of another kind may be necessary. While not all viral infections prove fatal, they do require professional attention so that they do not lead to other more serious diseases which can be fatal.

HAIRBALLS

Cats shed heavily during certain seasons and according to their environment. This condition can easily present problems in the form of hairballs that form in the stomach as a result of the cat's licking itself clean and ingesting the loose hair. Most cats throw up hairballs, while at times the condition might call for a mild laxative or the feeding of small lumps of white vaseline or a dose of mineral oil or Petromalt. There are also other lubricants to aid in passing hairballs through the cat.

Hairballs can be avoided by proper and diligent grooming, which should be done on an even more frequent basis during the changing of seasons when you notice the cats are shedding more than usual.

WORMS

Kittens are usually wormed before leaving the breeder, and it is not necessary to worm them again. If worms are found (after observing symptoms such as passing them, throwing them up, sudden loss of appetite, scruffy coat, runny eyes, showing a voracious appetite and then no appetite at all) ask your veterinarian to prescribe a proper dosage according to the age and weight of the kitten and for the specific type of worm.

The type of worm can be determined by taking a fecal specimen to the veterinarian's office in a glass jar labeled with your cat's name and your name and address.

ALLERGY

Cats can fall victim to allergies just as readily as people can. Some allergies might come from a reaction to carpeting, certain fabrics, plants (many house plants are fatal to both cats and dogs!) and foods. Symptoms are sneezing, watery eyes, rubbing the nose, or shaking the head.

Most common of the allergies among cats are the food allergies. Upset stomach and skin eruptions are a direct result of food allergy, and an immediate removal of the objectionable food is usually all that is necessary to clear up the condition. However, the difficulty might lie in establishing the necessary balanced diet to keep your cat healthy. It is wise to discuss any severe diet change with your veterinarian, and for skin irritations medication from him is also indicated. These may take the form of oral or injected medicants.

CYSTITIS

Space forbids mentioning all the known diseases to which a neglected cat may fall prey, but since cystitis is such an excruciatingly painful condition, and one, unfortunately, which is becoming more and more prevalent, we must mention it here, however briefly. Cystitis is especially common among male cats and can kill.

In simple terms cystitis is an acute or chronic inflammation of the bladder. The inflammation causes varying degrees of damage to the wall of the bladder, resulting in the formation and accumulation of organic debris. The normally acid urine then turns to alkaline, and salts which are normally soluble in urine turn into crystals. These crystals are often called "stones" or "plugs," which block the urethral passage, resulting in extreme difficulty in urination and excessive pain. Male cats, which have a much narrower urinary passage than females, are therefore especially susceptible.

This blockage results in the backing up of the urine into the kidneys, which prevents the removal of poisonous wastes from the cat, causing a condition known as uremia. Unless the blockage is relieved quickly, *a painful death results!* If you notice your cat lingering in the litter pan, making frequent attempts to urinate with little or no results, an immediate trip to the veterinarian is indicated. Time is of the essence.

Cystitis is seen in cats of all ages, and the exact cause is not yet known. Extensive research is being conducted to determine the likelihood that metabolic imbalance, viral infection or bacteria, dry food, fish, lack of vitamin A, etc., could be considered as possible causes. Meantime, make sure your cat drinks plenty of water and watch carefully for the onset of this painful condition.

PNEUMONITIS

The most common — because it is one of the most contagious — viral disease known to felines is pneumonitis.

Comparable to pneumonia in people, it is seldom fatal in itself but can be if constant care is not given to the afflicted cat. Cats do not eat when they cannot smell their food, and one of the most obvious symptoms of pneumonitis is a nose clogged with mucus. So, strange as it may seem, one of the dangers of the disease is that your cat may starve to death if you do not see to it that the nose is kept open at all times. This can be done with a moist tissue or swab and by putting dabs of Vaseline on the nose to prevent its drying and to make the cat lick its nose, allowing the congestion to be sneezed out.

The prime objective is to keep the cat eating and to administer regularly any medication the veterinarian prescribes after the initial injections of antibiotics he will undoubtedly administer. Other symptoms are fever, runny eyes and general listlessness.

RABIES

While rabies can hardly be classed as a "common ailment" with which this chapter deals primarily, we mention it here briefly because of its severity. Rabies is still the most feared and dreaded disease among pet owners, since there is still no known positive cure.

Rabies is also a viral disease transmitted through the saliva (usually by way of a bite) by all warm-blooded animals and humans. Madness and death are the ultimate results. House cats are seldom affected, but all cats permitted outdoors or exposed to rabbits, squirrels, foxes or bats should be inoculated. Many towns perform this service free of charge, and calling the local health department will usually provide information as to when and where the inoculation can be had.

A rabid cat will either attack or try to hide from people or other animals; it will try to drink but have difficulty in swallowing, and it might foam at the mouth and undergo a complete change in personality. The author had a rabid dog several years ago and had to undergo the complete series of injections in the Pasteur treatment for rabies. It was an almost unimaginably painful experience, and I would suggest it would be much wiser to take every known precaution against exposure to the disease than to have to tolerate the pain of the serum and the threat of madness and eventual death.

Chapter 14
CATS AND THE LAW

Just what legal rights do you have as a cat owner? What legal rights does your cat enjoy? Many strange stories have been told about the strange legal confrontations in the courts of our land as a result of the "minglings of man and beast." None are stranger or more ardent than those involving cats.

In today's modern world of practical applied breeding practices and the buying and selling of kittens and cats, we have learned to avoid legal entanglements to a large degree by drawing up simple contracts between the parties involved.

Generally speaking, there has been little conflict in the area of the privileges of cats that are allowed to roam free. In spite of the population explosion — in both the cat and human worlds — most of the towns in the United States have no restrictive laws on cats. This is not necessarily the case where apartment buildings are concerned.

Many apartment house owners are very successful in winning court cases where tenants that own cats can be evicted or refused rentals. While there is little threat of damage to an apartment — other than odor — many apartment owners do not want cats or any other pets at all in their buildings or on their premises, and they win their cases in court. This also applies whether or not there was a "no pets" clause in the lease, or whether or not there were complaints of any kind from the neighbors.

While a number of factors have conspired to cut down the number of cats allowed to roam free in cities, in the country, where cats are a necessity in the barns and fields, they are becoming more and more of a point of argument. While they are considered a necessity on one hand, the type and amount of damage they can do has become a topic of heated controversy in more recent years.

WILLS AND BEQUESTS

While most cases where cats are mentioned in wills or left bequests often involving large sums of money for their maintenance are upheld in court, they do cause a great deal of criticism from those who do not fully appreciate cats or the part the cat had played as a cherished companion of the deceased. We must remember that at certain periods during history they were thought to be of so little value that it was not considered a crime to steal them. Mistreatment of cats throughout history is well known in spite of the fact that they were worshiped in Egypt, and superstitions concerning cats have always been prevalent.

Fortunately, in many states it is now the law that anyone striking a cat or dog with an automobile must stop and not only report the incident, but whenever possible help the animal at the scene of the accident. A good step forward!

BELLING THE CAT

Off and on for years there has been a great deal of pro and con discussion regarding the licensing of cats, the insistence on their wearing collars, and especially of their wearing collars with bells on them to announce their presence on the scene. It had even been made "law" on some occasions to try out the theory. It did not work!

It did bring to mind, however, the famous statement made centuries ago in one of Aesop's fables: "Who is to bell the cat? Is is easy to propose impossible remedies."

The classic encounter between cat lovers and bird lovers was, I believe, settled for once and for all by the late Adlai Stevenson while he was governor of Illinois, his comments were the subject of an editorial I wrote; published in *CATS* magazine, September, 1965. It went like this:

ON ADLAI STEVENSON
Guest Editorial by Joan Brearley

THE DEATH OF Ambassador Adlai E. Stevenson

quite naturally brought to mind many fond recollections of the late Governor of Illinois. After listening to the various tributes paid to him both in print and on the radio and television I felt compelled as an animal lover in general, and a cat lover in particular, to reread one of his most quoted writings.

The occasion was his veto message to the Illinois Senate accompanying his return of a bill proposed by Illinois bird lovers and passed by both legislative houses in 1949. His message went as follows:

"To the Honorable, the Members of the Senate of the 66th General Assembly:

"I herewith return, without my approval, Senate Bill No. 93 entitled "An Act to provide Protection to Insectivorous Birds by Restraining Cats." This is the so-called "Cat Bill." I veto and withhold my approval from this bill for the following reasons:

It would impose fines on owners or keepers who permitted their cats to run at large off their premises. It would permit any person to capture, or call upon the police to pick up and imprison, cats at large. It would permit the use of traps. The bill would have statewide application — on farms, in villages, and in metropolitan centers.

"This legislation has been introduced in the past several sessions of the legislature, and it has, over the years, been the source of much comment—not all of which has been in a serious vein. It may be that the General Assembly has now seen fit to refer it to one who can view it with a *fresh outlook*. Whatever the reasons for passage at this session, I cannot believe there is a widespread public demand for this law or that it could, as a practical matter, be enforced.

"Furthermore, I cannot agree that it should be the declared public policy of Illinois that a cat visiting a neighbor's yard or crossing the highway is a public nuisance. It is in the nature of cats to do a certain amount of unescorted roaming. Many live with their owners in apartments or other restricted premises, and I doubt if we want to make their every brief foray an opportunity for a small game hunt by zealous citizens—with traps or otherwise. I am afraid this bill could only create discord, recrimination and enmity. Also consider the owner's dilemma: To escort a cat abroad on a leash is against the nature of the cat, and to permit it to venture forth for exercise unattended into a night of new dangers is against the nature of the owner. Moreover, cats perform useful service, particularly in rural areas, in combatting rodents—work they necessarily perform alone and without regard for property lines.

"We are all interested in protecting certain varieties of birds. That cats destroy some birds, I well know, but I believe this legislation would further but little the worthy cause to which its proponents give such unselfish effort.

Grand Champion Hima Tab Miss Muffet, pictured here as a five-month-old kitten. Owned by Mrs. LaVerne Grusell of Ashland, Ohio.

Harriet Himalayan and her friend Rita Rabbit. Himalayan owned by Rose Levy, Harobed Cattery; Rita Rabbit and photography by Sal Miceli.

The problem of cat versus bird is as old as time. If we attempt to resolve it by legislation, who knows but what we may be called upon to take sides as well in the age-old problems of dog versus cat, bird versus bird, even bird versus worm. In my opinion, the State of Illinois and its local governing bodies already have enough to do without trying to control feline delinquency.

"For these reasons, and not because I love birds the less or cats the more, I veto and withhold my approval from Senate Bill No. 93."

There can be no doubt that Mr. Stevenson was quite familiar with the strange nomadic ways of the cat, truly appreciated the fact that they did not recognize boundry lines, and that one of the most important instincts of the cat is its inherent desire to walk by night.

Chapter 15

GENERAL CAT CARE

ASSORTED HAZARDS AT HOME

Contrary to popular belief, cats do NOT always land on their feet! While they have an ability to land on all fours when jumping or falling from realistic heights, great care must be taken that they do not fall or drop from unusually high places. With more and more cats being kept as pets in highrise apartments, the rate of dead cats or broken bones as a result of falls from apartment terraces is alarming.

Cats can ususally handle themselves from heights found within a room, but porches, terraces and even tall trees can present a threat to their lives or mean broken bones or internal injury from falls.

Falls from windows where a cat has depended upon the screen as a brace are also a major threat to their lives. Each spring and fall the cat owner should check out the hooks on the screens and storm windows of the building to make sure they are secure.

The expression . . . "nervous as a long-tailed cat in a room full of rockers" is based on a long history of fact. Cats and kittens cannot be expected to determine the difference between a stationary chair and a rocker! Precautions should be taken if rocking chairs are in use to avoid paws and tails being crushed. Such injuries are painful, and bones are soft enough to be permanently damaged if run over at an early age.

The same applies to doors. Closet doors, cabinet doors, front and back doors — or car doors. All of them are a potential threat. Doors should not be left open for cats to get outdoors, and closets should not be left open for cats to get in, and then be locked in!

All animals should be kept out of the kitchen while cooking is in progress. Cats jumping on hot stoves or getting paws or tails caught in the refrigerator are more commonplace than we might imagine. Owners have been known to bump into a pot handle and spill hot food or liquid onto an animal. Feeding cats just before cooking is a good way to sate their appetite and keep them out of the kitchen.

SCRATCHING POSTS

While on the subject of furniture, let us discuss scratching posts. These paper or carpeted scratching posts, available at all pet shops and department stores, are almost essential to the cat owner who has any regard for upholstered furniture! Avoid catastrophe — buy a scratching post at the same time you buy your cat or kitten! Cats must scratch to sharpen their claws; they should have their claws to defend themselves.

DECLAWING CATS

While mentioning cats scratching on the furniture, quite naturally an alternative comes to mind: having the cat declawed. Dedicated cat fanciers do not approve of declawing cats, and you are not permitted to show a cat that has been declawed. It is also unfair and most unadvisable to declaw a cat that goes outside and must be equipped to defend itself. The only possible reason for declawing a cat is if it is a question of either keeping the cat or having it lose a good home! We must admit many lucky cats have gone to good homes when the owners were sure that the furniture would not be ruined. However, if the cat is declawed it is then the responsibility of the owner to give the necessary protection to that cat to insure its life and safety. Declawed cats should be kept indoors and not exposed to strange dogs or other animals.

Declawing is a painful operation and should be done by a veterinarian with experience at declawing. There is also the possibility that the claws may grow back.

Lovely headstudy of Patricia Kelly's Grand Champion Miss Sue of Kelly-Ko. This Tortie Point female carries the ideal color pattern for the Tortie Point. Ms. Kelly's Kelly-Ko Cattery is located in Pine Bush, New York.

LITTER PANS

Cats are born housebroken.

Kittens will learn very young the purpose of a litter pan. Almost as soon as they see one and feel the litter beneath their feet, they will instinctively know its purpose, especially if the mother cat has used the pan herself and her familiar odor has permeated the litter. However, it is better not to allow young kittens to have cat litter until you are sure they realize it's not merely for jumping into or taking it in their mouths.

Newspaper or paper towels can be used until the purpose of litter is firmly established in their minds.

Paper towels are expensive but keep the kittens cleaner, since newsprint from the newspapers rubs off! With cats that like to dig vigorously in the litter and scatter it around, a newspaper base with just a shallow layer of litter can be the answer.

Cats eliminate twice a day at least, so litter pans should be changed at least once a day. Some cats will not use a litter pan a second time, so if you find your cat is also going just outside the litter pan, you will have to be sure you clean the pan after each time it is used. If you don't your cat is liable to develop a bad habit. It is possible he will not only go outside the pan but also may find another spot in the house to use! A clean cat wants a clean pan.

Litter pans should be washed out with a mild disinfectant on a regular basis. Pet shops sell deodorant sprays and liners for the pans to be used in addition to the litter, so there is really no reason for odor to permeate your home or cattery. Whole male cats are more of a problem, of course, and require a deeper pan if they spray.

DANGEROUS TOYS

While cats — and especially kittens — love to play, they must be watched, because they will play with anything that catches their fancy! Some toys can be harmful to them. Cellophane, pins and needles, hairpins, cigarettes or cigar butts and paper clips are just a few of the dangerous playthings which can be found around the house. Even some of the commercial toys can be dangerous if parts of them come off or rip open after strenuous play. Rubber balls small enough to get caught in the throat are a most common threat to their lives. Rubber toys that shred if swallowed will stick to the lining of the intestine and can kill. Broken feeding dishes or Christmas tree ornaments can prove fatal, as can wooden toys that splinter.

No matter what the toys, make periodic checks to see that they are in good condition; and if not, replace them.

LEASH TRAINING

It is certainly *possible* to leash train a cat. When started young, or if a cat is restricted to a house and yet obviously wants to get outside, it will learn to tolerate a leash or harness.

A harness is the best and safest type of leash, but with show cats too much exercise on a harness can damage the coat. A soft leather rolled or round collar or a woven nylon lead is best for the show cat or longhaired cat. A harness or collar on the end of a long leash can allow a great deal of freedom of movement to the cat. It is unwise to tie a cat outdoors where it might slip out of the harness, get caught in shrubs or trees, or be subject to attack by other animals. A walk even once a day will provide ample exercise for the apartment or house cat not permitted to roam free.

Start kittens on the soft nylon leads and let them play with the lead at the same time they are getting used to the feel of it around their necks. Gradually begin to manipulate the lead to give them the feel of pressure and guidance; keep the walks very brief and very frequent in the beginning. Don't let them get bored so that they fight the lead or try to back out of it.

No matter how well your cat or kitten learns to walk on leash, do not expect these walks to become the time when the cat will relieve itself so that you may eventually eliminate a litter pan! This is where the similarity between walking a dog and walking a cat ends. While some cats will always perfer soft earth for digging and burying when they eliminate, you want them to always remember to use a litter pan when confined to the house . . . especially on cold or rainy days when you will find cats too sensible to want to go out of the house for *any* reason!

CAGING CATS

Far too many cats, especially show cats, live out their lives in cages. Too often these cages are in basements or catteries that are too large and impersonal to give each cat individual attention. Improper caging, such as cages that are too small

Ch. Pitts Apricot Brandy, Flame Point male with Grand Championship points. He has won Best and Second Best Himalayan several times. Owned by Michelle Woods, Palos Hills, Illinois.

and do not provide an interesting atmosphere, can destroy the true personality of the cat. The caging of some cats can actually endanger their physical development and general health if sufficient exercise is prevented by such confinement.

While cats adore crawling into paper bags, sleeping in closets, exploring attics and basement recesses, a cage with a closed door is something else again! If a cat must be caged, it must also have a period of time on a regular basis during which the cage door should be left open to give it the option to come and go as it pleases. In other words, the cat should be allowed to roam free at times to pursue its own desires and for a change of scene.

Eight-week-old Himalayan kitten Tomany Tribble and his Borzoi friend, at Mary Van Liew's Tomany Cattery in Kew Gardens, New York.

While show cats frequently must be caged to prevent damage to coat and mixed breedings and to provide a supervised diet, far too many show cats are never allowed to roam free indoors or outdoors and unfortunately bear the results of their confinement. It is almost obvious to all at the cat shows when this has been the case. So many of the show cats lack personality, stare at the audience with lackluster eyes or suddenly panic when they come into contact with part of the outside world. They "blow" at the slightest noise or become difficult to handle with strangers or even fear-bite when cornered in a cage that is not their own.

Confinement can have devastating effects on a cat's personality, and one of the most wonderful things about a cat is its personality — so if you don't intend to make the most of it, why have a cat at all!

CATS AND SUNLIGHT

Cats need sunshine and fresh air just as much as any other animal. Even if your cat is to be a show cat, it must get fresh air and sunshine, especially while it is growing up and developing. If your cat is caged but is at times allowed to run free in the house, be sure to provide an area outside where it can also spend some time in good weather. Put the inside cage on wheels which can be moved to an outdoor porch if a regular outside facility is not available. Some sort of an outside arrangement can easily be constructed and better still — build it around a tree so the cat can do its thing: climb!

Royal Merit and Quadruple Ch. Pittmans Duchess of Robrick photographed in October, 1974. This Blue Point female is pictured here at one-and-a-half years of age and has points toward her grand championship. The sire was R. M. Quadruple Ch. Chestermere Chiqulli *ex* Shawnee Blue Silk of Pittman.

THE FLEA COLLAR CONTROVERSY

My beloved veterinarian once said to me, "There is no disgrace in your cat's getting fleas, only in not getting rid of them!"

Sooner or later, if you have a cat, you will somewhere, somehow, pick up fleas. It can be at a cat show, a breeding, from a neighbor's cat strolling by or from any number of other methods which will afford the opportunity for the flea to hop onto your cat.

Over the years there have been any number of methods suggested to get rid of them . . . flea powders, medicated baths and so on. Pet shows offer shelves full of suggested remedies especially for the cat, since cats lick their fur in cleaning themselves and must have only the safest chemical applications applied!

In the 1970's the newest of all methods was popularized for getting rid of the pesky fleas, and it caused a great deal of controversy . At first it was welcomed with open arms . . . a collar that the cat wore, chemically treated to deter fleas and lasting for a period of a few months, when it could be replaced with a new one if necessary.

However, it was found to be highly irritating to some cats, causing irritation and swelling and soreness of the skin along with loss of hair. And it was especially irritating if it got wet. In more recent years the chemical aspect of the flea collar has been changed to make it more safe, and cat flea collars are now in common use.

Fleas can quickly ruin a longhair coat by the sheer need of the cat to scratch itself. Also, on the longhaired cat a collar that is worn constantly can also wear away the fur in that area. If your cat does get fleas you of course must get rid of the fleas, but only by using the method best suited to the cat. Powder for show cats, collar for household pets!!! But be on guard for any reaction your cat might have in addition to skin irritations, such as nausea, vomiting, diarrhea, or allergic reactions from the fumes which emanate from the chemical interior of the collar disk. If you notice anything out of the ordinary, see your veterinarian at once!

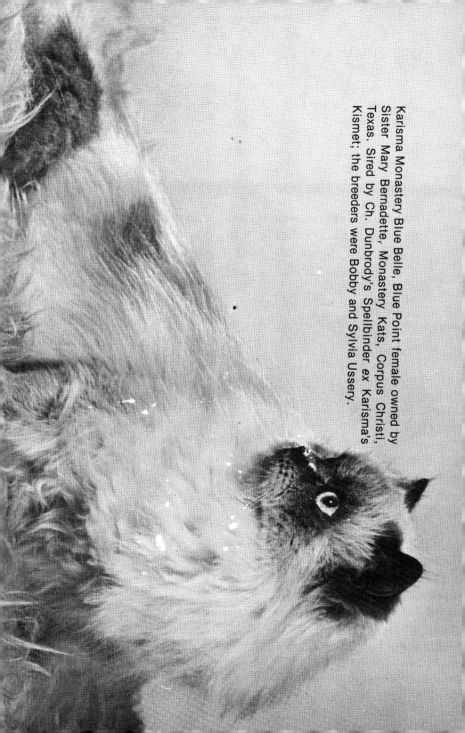

Karisma Monastery Blue Belle, Blue Point female owned by Sister Mary Bernadette, Monastery Kats, Corpus Christi, Texas. Sired by Ch. Dunbrody's Spellbinder ex Karisma's Kismet; the breeders were Bobby and Sylvia Ussery.

HOW NOT TO POISON YOUR CAT

So many house plants are poisonous to cats that it is almost impossible to list them all; it is safer to assume ALL plants are poisonous and keep them out of the house or at least out of the cat's reach! Hanging planters or miniature greenhouses are about the only sure way of accomplishing safety indoors.

Cats are also in danger from any disinfectant containing phenol or other chemicals used in both aerosol or liquid cleaners. Be sure to read labels before cleaning, especially around their living quarters. The newest threats along this line are the "toilet bowl cleansers." Any of these cleansers should be considered dangerous, since it is almost impossible to prevent cats or dogs from drinking out of the toilet. Be sure to read labels before purchasing your cleaning products to make sure they are safe for pets!

CAT BEDS

There are many charming and practical cat beds on the market and for sale in the shops; they are said to be perfect for cats. Many cats adore their own sleeping quarters and will welcome one of these plushy cubbyholes to curl up in on occasion. However, many cats will prefer to find their own favorite sleeping spot, and chances are it will be your bed with you in it, especially in winter time. If you are determined to keep the cat out of your sleeping quarters, put a bed for it in another room, lined with an old sweater or shirt of yours that will make it seem more like home.

Postscript

*"If man could be crossed with the cat
it would improve man, but it would
deteriorate the cat."*

— Mark Twain

INDEX